STUDIES IN MODERN EUROPEAN LITERATURE AND THOUGHT

General Editor:
ERICH HELLER
Professor of German
in the University College of Swansea

S T E F A N   G E O R G E

Other titles are in preparation

STEFAN GEORGE

BY

E. K. BENNETT

NEW HAVEN
YALE UNIVERSITY PRESS
1954

Printed in the United States of America

For
TERENCE WINDLE

CONTENTS

Introduction

Unlike his contemporaries Rilke and Thomas Mann, Stefan George has not excited great interest in the reading world outside his native country. Few translations of his poetry have appeared in English and only occasional essays have attempted an assessment of his place in modern European poetry. Even in Germany he has not yet been given his definite place in the order of its poets. For his importance has been much disputed, and like Helena in the second part of Goethe's *Faust* he appears as one greatly admired but also greatly blamed. The admiration and the blame have concerned themselves not merely with his poetry but with his personality, and the influence which his personality had upon his contemporaries. That his poetry is cold, mannered, too consciously willed, unmusical, is the charge brought against it by his detractors; whilst as a personality he has been charged with self-glorification, arrogance and the perversion of youth, now towards aestheticism, now towards Nazism.

A forceful and compelling personality may be an asset to a poet; it is not necessarily one. Considered in itself its drawback is that its greatest effectiveness can be felt only by those who come into immediate contact with it—a limited number of persons; the wider public knows of it only in so far as it is revealed in his poetry or—more debatably—through rumours and reports, and these tend on the whole to arouse aversion rather than sympathy. Thus there was a George-legend, the reaction to which was vaguely hostile among the general public in Germany before there was any wide-spread acquaintance with the poet's actual works. Some excuse for this hostile attitude to George amongst the general public may be found in the deliberate exclusiveness of the appeal which the poet made. Some years passed and a number of volumes had been printed before the actual publication of his works took place in the ordinary way. The earlier volumes were addressed to and accessible only to an élite. Only slowly and with the passing of years did George acquire a 'public' and that a restricted one, so that it can be said that his works never penetrated into the consciousness—far less the affection—of a wide public, nor indeed did he ever wish them to do so.

In 1914 when *Der Stern des Bundes* became to some extent the breviary of the young intellectuals who set forth to war, they were taking with them a book which was originally intended for a circle of initiates. Some of Rilke's works, notably the *Cornet* and *Die Geschichten vom lieben Gott*, became popular; no work of George's ever did. He had devotees—the immediate members of his circle—his avowed disciples; he had a certain limited public among the intellectuals who were convinced of his merits as a poet—a larger circle than that of his devotees; outside of that there was only an indifferent or even hostile world mainly of detractors. Only towards the very end of his life did George allow any of his poems to appear in anthologies—the most easy means of access to a poet. Nor did any selection of his poems in German appear until after his death. It may be said that in withholding his assent to such forms of publication George was wise, for his poems gain greatly by being read in their proper framework; and in the arrangement of each volume of his works the same principle of form is at work as in each individual poem.

Many books have been written on Stefan George in German by those who were actually members of his circle or those who were closely connected with it. They are not in the strict sense critical works. The personality of the poet impinges too greatly upon the writers' consciousness for a critical attitude to the poems to be possible for them. The principle of loyalty to the Master hampers any freedom of judgment. The poetry is accepted as great poetry and no detailed investigation of individual poems is attempted. Where references are made to other poets they are to Dante, Shakespeare and Goethe. It is tacitly assumed that George's place is with these. To assign him a place beside Platen or Conrad Ferdinand Meyer, with whom amongst German poets he has formally the greatest affinity, would seem little short of impiety. Yet, though he is unquestionably a greater poet than either of these, he is equally unquestionably of a lesser stature than Hölderlin. Some of the latest important writings on him are still written by those who actually knew him. There are, nevertheless, indications in the essays occasionally appearing in literary journals at present that there is a growing feeling, after some years of neglect, that the time has come for a more detached assessment of him, an assessment which can be made only by those who did not come under the immediate influence of his personality.

That he was a great and forceful personality there can be no doubt; that he was a man of the highest intellectual ability with an understanding and grasp of the problems of his age seems equally indubitable; that he was a great poet in the strictest sense of the word 'great' cannot so easily be maintained. And whether the atmosphere of grandeur which surrounded him can convincingly be preserved when those who knew him and helped to create it have passed away is even more problematical.

Stefan Anton George was born on the 12th July 1868, in Büdes-heim near Bingen on the Rhine, the son of a well-to-do owner of vineyards who afterwards owned a wineshop in Bingen itself. The family was peasant in origin, but the poet's father had be-come affluent enough to enable his son to devote his life to poetry without requiring of him that he should take up any of the accepted money-making professions. There seem to have been no parental conflicts: both father and mother accepted tacitly the way of life their son had chosen. After the usual school education George spent some time at the University of Berlin. But the years of travel, rather than university studies, completed an education based on the classical training of a German Gymnasium (Darmstadt) in the latter half of the nine-teenth century. From his childhood George had shown a great interest in words, and whilst still a child he invented a language of his own. Later in life he returned to this idea and carried it out more fully in a sort of *lingua franca*, which included Latin, Provençal, Catalan and Spanish elements; so fully indeed was this artificial language developed that he was able to use it for poetical composition, and two poems in *Der Siebente Ring* were originally written in it. The last two lines of the poem *Urspruenge* in the same volume are written in the language he invented as a child.

He was at home in many European languages; and his trans-lations of English, French, Italian and Spanish poetry, as well as his translations into English and French of his own poems, bear witness to his mastery of these languages.

His travels took him to London, where he spent some months, to France, Austria, Spain and Italy. His visits to France and to Austria have outstanding importance in the history of his career as a poet. In Paris he was introduced to the circle of Symbolist poets, and accepted from them the then prevailing Symbolist mode of poetry which determined his own develop-ment as a poet. In Vienna he made the acquaintance of the young Hofmannsthal, in whom he believed he had found a poet who confirmed him in his own conception of poetry. With him, however, he failed to establish a relationship on the lines which he wished.

At home in Germany, where the greater part of his life was spent, he lived for some years in Bingen in the house of his parents. Later his chief centres of residence were Berlin, Munich and Heidelberg, in each of which towns he had a *pied-à-terre*, usually only a single room, in which he lived and received his disciples. The last months of his life were spent in Italian Switzerland, whither he took refuge from his native country after it had passed under the rule of National Socialism. Here he died on the 4th December 1933.

George's mode of life as far as material things are concerned was sober and unpretentious. Though he had well-to-do and wealthy friends in whose homes he was made welcome, the rooms in which he lived were furnished in a severe style, which eschewed any attempt at luxury. His dress, though departing sufficiently from the regular mode of male fashion to make him a somewhat conspicuous figure, was likewise severe and formal. Not only in that, however, but also in the dignity of his figure and of his lineaments he commanded attention and respect. If there was affectation in the way he presented himself to the outward world, it was the affectation of simplicity, not of ostentation, and the severity of line which is one of the characteristics of his poetry was also a characteristic of his whole visible being. Those who knew him, even those whose acquaintance with him was merely transient, testify to the arresting effect upon them of his appearance, his glance, his speech. It may be said, and has been said, that these effects were deliberately cultivated; but it must in justice be admitted that nature had endowed him with the materials from which to create his effects, and that in the cultivation of them he was essentially proceeding along the course which she had laid out for him. By following that course both in his life and in his poetry he preserved the integrity of a personality controlled and ordered by the unity of a positive idea. He was, in fact, in his personality, his mode of life and his poetry, 'all of a piece'.

A personality of force communicates himself, when a poet, not merely by the written word, but also by immediate contact with other personalities, who are in sympathy with him and receptive of his ideas and conception of life. The more compelling he is as a personality the greater will be his authority and hold over those whom he gathers up in the circle of his intimacy; the greater his conviction and assurance of the rightness and importance of his ideal, the more selective he will be in choosing those to whom he communicates himself, and the closer and more demanding will be his union with them. George's contact with the world of men was primarily through the circle of friends whom he had chosen as being in sympathy with his ideals, men whose relationship with him was that of disciples to their master or leader. Hofmannsthal was to have been the first of those disciples, but would not accept the rôle.

It is this position of George as a leader and teacher surrounded by a devoted circle of disciples which all his life placed him at one remove from contact with ordinary humanity. It is as though he could be reached only through the medium of his disciples, to whom in the first place his words were addressed, for whom primarily his personality existed, and by whom his poems were more immediately comprehended. What is known of him as a man, the significance of some of his later obscurer poems, the esoteric wisdom which they contain, must pass through the minds of his disciples before it can be understood by the outside world. No other poet has worked quite in this way; but it is characteristic of George. The circle around him began to form very early in his career as a poet, and the printing of the first number of *Die Blätter für die Kunst* (1892) gave the first tangible evidence of the existence of such a band of men whose unity consisted in their acceptance of the ideas of one central and controlling personality. In the early days they were men of George's own age, and many of them remained faithful to him to the end of their lives; but as the years passed and George grew older, they were selected from younger generations, and the circle which surrounded the ageing George consisted largely of talented and promising youths and young men, together with a number of the old stalwarts from earlier generations.

The circle of young men around George—*der George Kreis*, as it was known in Germany—may perhaps be described as an assembly of men of intellectual interests and ability which had something in common with the group of poets who enjoyed the intimacy of Mallarmé and were habitual visitors in the Rue de Rome, and something in common with the circle of young men who surrounded Socrates as described in the Platonic dialogues. The *Kreis* partook of the nature of both, but differed from either. In its earlier days it was concerned more especially with the discussion and promulgation of new ideas of poetry, and manifested itself in the printing of the early numbers of *Die Blätter für die Kunst*. But the influence of George upon it was more authoritarian than that of Mallarmé upon the habitués of the Rue de Rome, or of Socrates upon the young men of Athens, for though some attached themselves to Socrates more closely, his interest in them claimed no absolute adherence to any doctrines as a requirement. But like the attitude of Socrates, the attitude of George to his disciples was in essence a paedagogic one, and as time went on and the difference in age between the Master and his followers became necessarily greater, the paedagogic element emerged more clearly.

It was not merely a conception of poetry which the disciples were required to share with the Master, but a conception of

13

life; and what had originally been an aesthetic training (in which indeed ethical elements were already present) became ultimately a more explicitly ethical one, in which order, measure, discipline and the idea of a dedicated life were the qualities stressed. Membership of this group was not easily obtained, though the Master was on the look-out for suitable candidates. (Boehringer in his book *Mein Bild von Stefan George* gives an account of George's mistaken decision with regard to the admission of one apparently suitable candidate, which is not without its humorous side.) Once incorporated in the circle, absolute loyalty was demanded of the members; and though the suggestion of tyranny is firmly repudiated by those who were members, to the outside public the attitude of George may easily appear to have been tyrannical, at least autocratic. Some members broke away; differences of opinion upon matters of importance led to exclusion—marriage, for instance, might be construed as a breach of loyalty to the Master; friction between individual members might lead to the expulsion of one or more; the publication of a work of learning which did not meet with George's approval called down severe reproof upon the author. To George's credit it must be said that the attitude of Anti-Semitism in some of his disciples was one of the causes which led to the most violent upheaval in the history of the circle.

The *Kreis* aroused in the minds of the inadequately informed general public disapproval and derision; sometimes specific charges were made against it, for instance that it alienated young men from their parents and homes; on the whole, it was regarded as an assembly of affectedly superior and fantastically minded youths who had placed themselves under the domination of a pretentious and not very highly approved poet who was both in his poetry and in his life something of a charlatan. In truth it would seem that what had originally been an organic growth, the natural development from the seed of one forceful personality who had attracted around himself companions who shared his views and in a lesser degree his gifts in aesthetic matters, had hardened into something more artificial and self-conscious.

But underlying the formation of the circle, and the foundation of the journal *Die Blätter für die Kunst*, is a principle which unites in a general idea the seemingly so disparate poems of the younger and the elder George—the idea of a mission. Obscured to some extent by the aestheticism of the early poems, it is nevertheless there, though it does not emerge clearly until the publication of *Der Siebente Ring*. To the young George the cultural decay of his time was already apparent—apparent most

14

pressingly in German poetry, for the poetry of an age was for him the key to the civilization of the age itself. Others were equally aware of the decay of civilization; and the German Naturalists, whose earliest works appeared at the same time as the earliest works of George, manifested their disapproval of contemporary German literature and life in their plays, novels and to a lesser degree their lyrical poetry. But the form and methods of their reaction were not such that George could partner or even accept them. Where they revolted against contemporary literature because of its triviality and the remoteness in subject matter from the problems of the day, George was in revolt against the carelessness, the neglect of formal beauty which characterized the German poetry popular in his youth. The question of formal beauty was not one which had any part in the Naturalists' aim to create a new type of literature. Their methods and preoccupations were to George merely a further indication of the degeneracy of contemporary poetry. He abhorred them. To give to poetry a new purity, a perfection of form; to restore the Word to an innocence and clarity lost in the careless traffic to which it had been subjected by writers who had not realized their responsibility to the sacred instrument it was their duty to preserve; this was the aim, the obligation imposed upon him, his mission, to which he devoted himself more exclusively in his early works. Poetry, in Germany, had for George lost its dignity, its sanctity; it was his task to restore it to its high estate.

George's reaction to the decay of civilization which surrounded him was not to put forward plans for the reformation of the world—*Weltverbesserungspläne* are rejected as the subject matter of poetry in the early numbers of *Die Blätter für die Kunst*—but to create for himself a mode of life which in itself would be the exemplary realization of his protest against the prevailing sloth of the spirit. 'To make', as Eric Gill wrote, 'a corner of good living in the chaos of the world'. The regeneration of poetry with which he began would imperceptibly bring about the regeneration of society: the circle of young men who assembled around him would automatically, having imbibed the ideas of the Master, form a league of youth to carry these ideas out into the world and so bring about a new order of life. Though the theoretical statement of aims in the earliest numbers of *Die Blätter für die Kunst* was exclusively concerned with the regeneration of poetry, as the title of the journal suggested, by the end of the century a contributor (it may not have been George himself, for the prose contributions are unsigned) could write, no doubt too optimistically, of the generation which had been

15

nourished on the ideas of the Master: that the light of Hellas had descended upon the youth of our age, inspiring them with an ardent aspiration for a life in which beauty manifests itself in the body and in the mind as the principle of proportion, causing them to reject the shallow culture of the day and the outmoded barbarism of the past; and, neither rigid in their uprightness nor ignoble in their submissiveness, to advance through life with heads erect, recognizing themselves as members of a great people and not of one individual tribe among many.

It seems clear therefore that in spirit the influence of George within his circle by this time was more akin to that of Socrates than that of Mallarmé. George's ideal was that of the controlled life. In the chaos and abandonment of contemporary civilization he aimed at the establishment of an example of individual life in which the soul, the spirit and the body were combined in a harmonious unity of co-operation and control. George was brought up in the Catholic faith, and of it he retained the sense of discipline. But fundamentally he drew his inspiration from the ideas of classical antiquity. In *Der Teppich des Lebens* the Angel who brings him the message of his life contrasts the accept-ance of Christian ideals with that of Greece; and whilst admitting the validity of the former for the great mass of mankind, claims for a smaller select group allegiance to the faith of Hellas. Upon their banners is inscribed the watchword: 'Hellas ewig unsre liebe'.

The 'third humanism', as it is sometimes designated, dis-penses with a transcendental god and places the godhead in man himself. In this humanism George reveals a spiritual arrogance greater than that of any other writer. The dead god for whom, with Nietzsche, the substitute is to be found in the future in the Superman, is for George a living god still, is in the present, is embodied in man. Man is the criterion and measure of all things, which have interest and significance for George only in so far as they minister to man. It is man who, as in Goethe's poem *Das Göttliche*—which is a glorification of man, not of the gods— distinguishes, selects and judges, who can give eternal duration to the moment. Control is for George a function of power. Under-lying the idea of control is the aspiration, the prerogative of power; the insistent urge to bring life, and not merely the poet's own ethical life, under his spiritual control. All that cannot be brought under this dominion, that has not been shaped (*gestal-tet*) by the spirit of man, arouses in George misgivings, suspicion, alarm. It is an alien realm to him with which he cannot or will not become familiar. He is Apolline, and turns away with distaste from the Dionysian. All that partakes of the Dionysian or

16

orgiastic is hostile to the creation of that ordered, controlled and formed existence which was in some degree his achievement as well as his aspiration.

Thus his attitude to nature, to which he is insensitive except in so far as it is humanized by the presence of man in it. Sabine Lepsius[1] records the strange feeling she had, when walking with George in the country, that he seemed to be out of place, to be in an element which was alien to him; and in the immediately following incident of the infant child which turned from him in terror, she widens the significance of her original feeling to suggest that wherever nature manifested itself in its spontaneous and uncontrolled being George was a stranger. Nature is for him, one may say, always landscape background; its existence in its own right is a disturbing aspect of it to be ignored if possible or at least passed over in silence. The poem *Urlandschaft* in *Der Teppich des Lebens*, which apparently glorifies a primaeval landscape, is in reality a manifestation of this attitude of mind towards nature, for the poem, as its last lines reveal, is in fact not a celebration of primaeval landscape but of its elimination as such by the irruption into it of the human pair:

> Des ackers froh des segens neuer mühn
> Erzvater grub erzmutter molk
> Das schicksal nährend für ein ganzes volk.[2]

Mankind has, in fact, taken possession of nature and is preparing to take it under control and exploit it for its own purposes. Even George's attitude to nature as the source of all life, envisaged as a female figure, the nourisher of existence, brooding in the depths of being over the springs from which all life flows, is one of control, transformed into compulsion if she be recalcitrant to man's will:

> Und wenn die grosse Nährerin im zorne
> Nicht mehr sich mischend neigt am untern borne ⁄
> In einer weltnacht starr und müde pocht:
> So kann nur einer der sie stets befocht

> Und zwang und nie verfuhr nach ihrem rechte
> Die hand ihr pressen ⁄ packen ihre flechte ⁄

[1] Sabine Lepsius and her husband were friends of George in Berlin and promoted an interest in his poetry. The incident is recorded in her book, *Stefan George, Geschichte einer Freundschaft* (1935).
[2] English translations of quoted passages, which are by the author throughout, will be found in the Appendix on page 59.

Dass sie ihr werk willfährig wieder treibt:
Den leib vergottet und den gott verleibt.

The poem, *Templer*[1], in which these lines occur is highly revealing. The sacred band of young men is acclaimed, an ideal fellowship it is true, but one which recalls the disciples of George. All the immemorial deeds and necessary changes which the world requires are performed by men who are members of this fellowship. And not only in the world of action do they impose their will, but upon the order of human life as determined by nature. If nature should refuse to carry on her task in some dark period of the world, only one who has constantly combatted her and exercised compulsion upon her and never has proceeded in accordance with her laws is able to force her to pursue her task obediently. But what is her task? It is, as George enunciates it: to deify the body, and make bodily the deity. The final step has been taken, both in the exercise of control and in the separation from nature. Her task has been imposed upon her, not by God but by man. George's fundamental obsession with power, expressed even in his ideal of a highly disciplined personal life, stands openly revealed. The ideal of humanism has been exalted to a supreme, magnificent but impious height. The superman has been realized. Man, nature and God have been subjected to human compulsion.

II

If the words 'obsession with power' be used, however, the idea (so frequently imputed to George) must be guarded against that this is in any way connected with political ideas, and that it implies any belief in the ideas of German aggrandizement or in the achievements of the second Empire. It is in the world of the spirit that his power rules. His attitude to the Germany of his day, to its political and economic ambitions, its satisfaction with the state of culture attained, is at least as contemptuous as that of Nietzsche in *Unzeitgemässe Betrachtungen*. The word Prussian, describing in any sense George's attitude of mind, is singularly out of place, as is apparent in the partially destroyed poem entitled *Bismarck*, in which his abhorrence and contempt for all that Prussia stood for were so plainly stated that he felt it unwise to publish it. The *Templer* of the poem, the body of

[1] In *Der Siebente Ring*. The substance of the lines is given in this and the preceding paragraph.

young men whose achievements are the imperishable acts and turning points in the history of the world, form an ideal brotherhood. They move about their affairs in silence on paths which are not acclaimed by fame; they have been nurtured in remote regions; their successors are not of the same tribe as they are; they are denizens of the wide world and not of any particular country. Theirs is a universal brotherhood of men, united by a common heroic spirit, not of men united in some definite organization. Indeed all organizations which sought to unite men, to bring them into subjection to some mass community, not least the youth organizations prevalent in George's later years under the name of *Wandervögel* or *Jugendbewegungen*, were highly distasteful to him. It was to the individual that he addressed himself, and upon whom he sought to exercise his influence, impressing upon each an aristocratic ideal of life, rejecting the, for him, false ideals of democracy. For him the idea of the leader and his followers was fundamental. But the followers were intimately connected with the leader and the relationship was a personal one; a mass following was repugnant to him. That there were dangers in this idea is evident. Questionable above all is the requirement of absolute loyalty of the disciple to the leader, at least as long as man remains a fallible being. But loyalty is a good and beautiful thing in itself, and should not be denigrated because it can be perverted to ignoble and evil ends. The mass application of the principle was something which George did not envisage, and when it occurred, slavish, uncritical and utilized for the promulgation of ideas which he abhorred, he turned aside from it with that nausea which is naturally aroused by caricature of something deeply cherished.

Similarly the idea that George glorified war as something 'holy' is mistaken. It is based upon a phrase quoted out of its context in a poem in *Der Stern des Bundes*. The poem begins with an indictment of those who, in their *hubris*, sought to erect an ever higher edifice of vainglory; now threatened by its collapse they are afraid of suffocating under its ruins. Too late, the prophet exclaims: madness, pestilence and war will destroy them in their thousands and tens of thousands. It is here that the word '*heilig*' occurs, applied equally to madness, pestilence and war. It is used in the sense of belonging to the gods, not as a blessing bestowed upon man, but as a dire fate which impends over him.

In 1906, when the political situation in the Balkans seemed to make war inevitable, Hofmannsthal wrote to George asking his help in persuading the leading literary men in Germany and England to sign an appeal for lasting peace between the two

19

countries. George refused. But these were the reasons he gave: 'War is only the final result of senseless activities which for years have recklessly been directed towards it. The attempt of a few individuals to plaster over the breach seems to me to have no effect.'

It seems necessary to clear away these crude charges against George. They are based upon an inadequate familiarity with his actual writings, and have their origin not in the words which he actually wrote, but in the legend which was the creation of ignorance and hostility. There is doubtless much that is open to criticism in the ideals and the methods of George, but the ideal was that of 'das schöne Leben', in which the conflicting elements in the nature of man were brought into harmony, and were allowed to function in beauty under the control of the spirit. In his idea of the good life neither the glorification of war nor material ostentation and national aggrandizement nor a complacent acceptance of democracy could play a part; indeed these were felt to be its most obvious enemies.

III

When George turned his attention to the writing of poetry in the later eighties of the century, the great lyric impulse in German poetry coming from Goethe had reached its end, stung to death by the irony of Heine. The tradition of 'Gefühlslyrik'—the immediate expression of feeling—still continued, but its practitioners were minor poets whose sentimentalities merely reiterated themes and emotions which the earlier poets had exhausted. The popular writers of lyrics were castigated in the literary essays *Kritische Waffengänge* of the Brothers Hart, which appeared in the middle of the decade. The only lyric poet of any originality and stature was the Swiss Conrad Ferdinand Meyer, the precursor of the symbolic lyric in German literature. And it is significant that in the anthology of German lyric poetry made by George later, Meyer is the only writer of the second half of the century who is included. George's poems written before 1890, and considered by him merely as prentice work, were not collected and published until 1901, and appear now under the title of *Die Fibel* (*The Hornbook*) as the first volume of the collected works.

It was, as has already been indicated, George's visit to Paris in 1889, his meeting with the Symbolist poet Albert de Saint Paul, and through him his acquaintance with the group of Symbolist poets of whom Mallarmé was the centre, which determined for George the type of poem he was to write, and evoked in him a conscious acceptance of their methods. 'A conscious acceptance'; for it is with George, in whom all is deliberate, not merely the question of an influence unconsciously imbibed, but of a decision taken. Unpremeditatedness, whether in song or in life itself, is not a characteristic of George. Indeed a deliberate reaction against the all too unpremeditated or not sufficiently premeditated poetry of his German contemporaries was part of his own poetic impulse—if impulse be the right name for something in which the functioning of the will played so important a part. But the methods of the French Symbolists were not accepted without certain modifications on the part of George, so that in a comparison of his poems with those of his French contemporaries it will be seen that there was no question of slavish imitation. In some respects indeed, in the actual handling of his subject matter, George reveals a kinship with Conrad Ferdinand Meyer.

A brief survey of French poetry at the time will show George's divergence and originality. When he came under the influence of French poetry the vogue of Parnassianism was already past. The Elephants of Leconte de Lisle had lumbered across the endless plains and had at last disappeared; and though, no doubt, the Condor was still planing over the Andes it too was lost to sight. The period in which it was considered to be the function of poetry to give an exact picture of objective nature was now over, and the Symbolists who had superseded the Parnassians aimed at giving only so much of external nature as was necessary to constitute a symbol for the *état d'âme* of the poet which was to be communicated. The result was that precise description was no longer required nor desired, and that objective lineaments were dissolved into movement, vagueness and imprecision with a marked tendency towards achieving musical rather than plastic effects. This went together with a general lack of concern about the exact comprehensibility of a poem. Suggestion and evocation were the demands of the French Symbolists. Mallarmé speaks of the new art of poetry as rejecting the material objects of nature, and of a direct thought which gives order to them, as something brutal. It is the horror of the forest and not the dense trees of which the forest is composed which the poet can hope to enclose within his volume. But George, in so far as he desires a renewal of German poetry, is faced with a different situation. 'For in France', as Carl August Klein wrote, 'the perfection of Parnassianism, to which we have not attained, has been abandoned'. With this realization George sets out to combine elements inherent in both types of poetry; Parnassian

21

strictness of form and precision of line with the more fluid movement of the Symbolists. But there are also other divergences from his Symbolist models. He never made use of free rhythms because the very name seemed to him a contradiction in terms, a denial of the element of form. He wrote: 'Free rhythms is as much as saying white blackness: he who cannot move in rhythm should confine himself to prose. The strictest measure is at the same time the greatest freedom'. He rejected also the tendency to be unconcerned about the comprehensibility of a poem. Klein, who often enunciates the underlying principles of George's poems, where George is content to let the poems speak for themselves, wrote: 'In contrast to the youngest generation [he is referring to the youngest school of French poets] who dissolve the forms, his are strictly regular, never lacking comprehensibility and the disciplined concentration which gives a clear outline to the whole'. In later years George declared his debt and gratitude to the French poets of his youth in the poem *Franken*: [1]

> Es war am schlimmsten kreuzweg meiner fahrt ...
> Hier die gemiednen gaue wo der ekel
> Mir schwoll vor allem was man pries und übte ⁄
> Ich ihrer und sie meiner götter lachten.
> Wo ist dein dichter ⁄ arm und prahlend volk?
> Nicht einer ist hier.

Disgusted with the civilization of his own country he turned to France, and found there 'en France dulce Terre' the things which were dear to him, signalizing by name the writers Villiers de l'Isle Adam, Verlaine and Mallarmé. When his first slight volume of poems entitled *Hymnen* appeared, his adherence to the principles and methods of the French Symbolists was apparent, while the underlying principles of poetry in accordance with which he was to work were set forth in the early numbers of *Die Blätter für die Kunst*. These statements in prose of the aims and ideals of the group of young men who shared George's ideas were possibly not all written by George himself, for it was his conviction that the renewal of German poetry should be manifested in actual poems rather than in statements of what it was or aimed at being. But since they find a place in the journal it must be assumed that George approved them as constituting, even if in fragmentary form, the manifesto of the new school of poetry of which he was the main represent-

[1] In *Der Siebente Ring*.

ative. The first number contains the following announcement of policy:

> The name of this publication announces already in part what its aims are: to serve art, especially poetry and letters, whilst excluding all that has reference to the state and society.
>
> It desires an art of the mind—an art for art's sake. Therefore it stands in contrast to that outmoded and second-rate school which had its origin in a mistaken conception of reality; it cannot, further, concern itself with world reforms and dreams of happiness for all in which at present the source of all that is new is seen; these may be very beautiful but they belong to spheres other than that of poetry.
>
> We consider it a merit that we do not begin with precepts, but with actual works of poetry which will illustrate our intentions and from which later the rules may be derived.

It is thus from the outset an art of the mind which is demanded, one in which it is essential, in the reader as well as the poet, that the mind should co-operate. This requirement is fulfilled by the poetry of George: the mind of the reader must be at work if he is to derive any satisfaction from it. But this does not mean that poetry must be the expression of thought. George writes: 'A poem is not the reproduction of a thought, but of a mood [*stimmung*]'; and again: 'We do not desire the invention of stories but the reproduction of moods; not reflection but presentation; not entertainment but impression'. This principle is maintained consistently in all George's poems, even in the hortatory poems in the later volumes. Again: 'the worth of a poem is determined—not by the meaning, otherwise it would be wisdom, instruction,—but by the form'.

Thus from the beginning stress is laid upon form, which is apprehended as a severe discipline. But discipline and form do not exclude the element of song which is an essential of poetry; and the importance of the musical element in poetry is signalized in the following statement: 'The deepest insight, the strongest impression are still no guarantee of a good poem. Both must first be transposed into the vocal tune which demands a certain tranquillity or even joy. That explains why every poem is unreal which conveys black without a ray of light.' One of the charges made against the poetry of George is that it lacks music. That charge has been denied by Sir Maurice Bowra, who claims for the poetry of George a greater quality of music than is to be found in the poems of Lenau and Mörike, the accredited masters

23

of music in German lyrical poetry. The claim may be felt to be exaggerated; the earlier and later poets do not differ in degrees of music; the difference is one of mode. A Gregorian chant is as much music as an anthem by Mendelssohn; and in contrast to Brentano, Lenau and Mörike, the music of George has a severer tone. Even of the poems which George entitles *Lieder* it may be said that the movement of the melody is stately rather than lively; it processes, it does not dance.

The symbolical nature of George's poetry is adumbrated in the following passages:

> The symbol is as old as language and poetry themselves. Individual words can be symbols, individual parts of a work as well as the complete content of an artistic creation may be a symbol. This last is also called the deeper significance which is inherent in every important work of art.

> To see the symbolical significance is the natural outcome of intellectual maturity and depth.

In later prose contributions to *Die Blätter für die Kunst* criticisms and objections made against it are refuted or explained away, but throughout the twenty-seven years of its existence it maintained unmodified the standpoint which it had taken up in its first number.

Twelve series (*Folgen*) of the *Blätter* appeared between the years 1892 and 1919, each series consisting of five numbers, the later series appearing less regularly than the earlier ones. George contributed both prose and verse. Prose passages, except those by George himself, were in the earlier numbers unsigned. His own comprised appreciations of German writers of the past (Jean Paul), cameos of descriptive writing, and a preface to his *Maximin*. All of his prose output which he selected for publication is contained in the seventeenth volume of the complete edition of his works, and bears the title *Tage und Taten*. It contains less than a hundred pages. In spite of the declared intention in the earlier numbers of the *Blätter* to eschew the statement of precepts and reflections, these elements creep in to some extent in the passages headed 'Merksprüche und Betrachtungen' which appear unsigned in its pages. But by far the greatest number of pages are devoted to poems, and pride of place is given to those of George himself. Extracts from volumes not yet published made their first appearance here, and these will be considered in due course. But apart from the poems of George and those of Hofmannsthal which are printed in the early *Folgen*, and a few by Dauthendey, the contributions are by poets whose names are not likely to figure largely in the history of German lyrical poetry, though some of them (Wolfskehl, for instance) are known today to discriminating circles of readers.

George's choice of the poems which he considered worthy of publication was highly individual, and was determined by what he called 'das Niveau' (the level) which would appear to have meant conformity with his principles of excellence of form and diction and a proper respect for the dignity of poetry: in short the acceptance of the attitude that poetry must be, in the old significance of the term, 'poetical' and preserve a poetical atmosphere. It is the poetry—to name a few of the accredited English poets who were contemporary—of Ernest Dowson (some of whose poems George translated), Lionel Johnson, William Watson, Laurence Binyon and perhaps even Stephen Phillips. Of course the contributions of George himself and those of Hofmannsthal (many of the most exquisite of his early poems) are of a higher standard than those of some of their English contemporaries mentioned; but in the poems which fill the greater number of the pages, poems by little-known or today entirely unknown poets, there is a frequent apostrophizing of the poet's lute or lyre, swans glide over dark waters, the poet's fate is deplored or extolled. The titles of many poems greet the reader's eye with a sense of familiarity: *Salambo*; *Herodias*; *Ariadne*; *Persephonia*; *Kalypso*; *König Kofetua und die Bettlerin*; whilst a whole world of troubadour romanticism is concentrated in the title *Wie ein edler Sänger sang und wie eine schöne Dame darauf starb*.

It is difficult to see how the regeneration of German poetry was to be brought about by the example of the poems judged worthy of publication in *Die Blätter für die Kunst*, except in so far as they were models of careful and clean workmanship and thus were a living reproach to careless and slipshod writing; and this was admittedly part of the reform of German poetry which George and those who shared his convictions were undertaking. George was intransigent in his rejection of the poetry by his contemporaries which did not conform to his own conception of what it should be. Thus he referred to that of Richard Dehmel, a poet whose work was highly rated at that time and is still accorded a respectable place in the history of German literature, as 'Dreck'. And the friendly relations with Dehmel on the part of one of the few women with whom George stood in some sort of familiarity caused him to break off all acquaintance with her. In his personal relations as in his attitude to

25

poetry George was ruthless. Even in the prose passages in the *Blätter* not by George himself, there is often a sweeping condemnation of much that sets itself up as having cultural value in German literature of the day; such statements, for instance, as: 'The fact that there is no possibility in Germany of an artistic or poetical event is a proof that we live in a cultural state of the second rank', or that neither in Switzerland nor in the northern countries could works be offered to the public as cultural achievements such as are offered in Germany.

IV

In the history of German poetry the name of Platen stands for the cultivation of formal beauty in verse. As such he is acclaimed and revered by those later poets and schools of poets who have stressed the importance of form; and as such he is quoted with approval and respect by George; indeed George sometimes couples his name with that of Goethe. He was attacked by Heine in a prose work entitled *Die Bäder von Lucca* in the twenties of the nineteenth century, an attack in which there is much that is scurrilous and concerned with him as a personality. But in the following passage an attempt is made by Heine—who is representative of an antithetical conception and practice of poetry —to define certain characteristics of Platen as a poet, and this has its bearing upon George as well. It should be noted that Platen was much concerned with poetry in set forms and with metrical complications, and that the excessive preoccupation with these elements in the art of poetry was repugnant and, one may feel, incomprehensible to Heine, so that where he found it he was apt to reject the works in which he felt it to be obtrusive. He writes:

> Though the muses are not favourable to Platen, yet he has the genius of language in his power, or rather he knows how to do violence to it . . . The deeper notes of nature, as we find them in folk songs, in children and in other poets have never burst forth from the soul of Platen . . . The anxious compulsion which he has to impose upon himself in order to say anything, he calls 'a great deed in words'—so utterly unknown to him is the very nature of poetry that he does not understand that the Word is a 'deed' only with the rhetorician, and that with the poet it is an 'event'. Language has never become the master in him as it has in the real poet; on the contrary it is he who has become master in language or rather

26

of language, like a virtuoso on his instrument. The greater the advance he made in the direction of technical skill, the greater was the opinion he had of his virtuosity; his skill extended over every form, he could versify the most difficult passages, he often, one may say, wrote poems on the G string.

The distinction between two types of poet adumbrated in the above passage is a real one, though exaggerated here by Heine. Nor is true poetry, as Heine suggests, the prerogative of the type of poet to which he belongs and from which Platen is so categorically excluded. But it is clear that George stands on the same side as Platen, Conrad Ferdinand Meyer and Théophile Gautier; whilst in the world of French contemporary poetry many of George's friends belonged there too. Defined as Heine defines it in respect of Platen, the function of the poet is to be the *master* of the word (pronouncements of Oscar Wilde claim the same achievement for himself in regard to words, i.e. lord of language), not its *minister*. That George's attitude to language falls into line with the whole trend of his nature becomes immediately apparent. Like Platen he doubtless approved and took to heart the *Venetian Epigram* which Goethe coined to stigmatize his countrymen: 'Eine Kunst nur treibt er und will sie nicht lernen: die Dichtkunst'. It was precisely against the unpremeditated outpourings of those poets who would not recognize that poetry was, as Novalis said, 'eine strenge Kunst', that Platen, and sixty years later George, undertook a campaign on behalf of correctness of form and selectiveness of language, with the recognition that poetry like every other art had to be learned before it could be practised with propriety.

A natural corollary to this insistence upon the formal and stylistic elements in poetry is the preoccupation with the choice of words, which implies generally a rejection of the current vocabulary and a preference for words which are not in normal usage. 'Donner un sens plus pur aux mots de la tribu' may be interpreted in two ways. The more correct way would seem to be to use the words of every day speech, but in such a way that their inherent meaning is not obscured by the careless and trite application of them. In this sense it may be said that Heine has claims to be considered a master if only an intermittent one, for he is able to take even the cliché and endow it with a significance which it does not possess in the mouth of the general public. Another way is that which was taken by Klopstock, Platen, Meyer and George in German poetry, namely to substitute for the generally used word one which for some reason or other has a loftier, usually more recondite quality, sometimes even a

periphrastic turn of phrase, as in Klopstock's odes 'Brot' becomes 'des Halmes Frucht', and 'Schlittschuh' 'Wasserkothurn'.
George carries this second procedure further than any of his
predecessors, and it adds to the difficulty in the understanding
of his poems to find words which are both recondite and archaic
(though doubtless linguistically justified). Nor can it be asserted
that these esoteric words are in themselves necessarily more
beautiful than the everyday words for which they are substitutes.
(Thus it would be difficult to maintain that 'blust' is more
euphonious than 'blüte'.) But their presence serves to produce
the air of guarded aloofness which invests his poetry: an air
which is heightened by yet other methods, calculated to keep
the domain of poetry within an enclosure which is separated
from actual life. George did not wish to make it easy of access; it
was a *hortus inclusus*, which was open only to those who were
prepared to make an effort to reach it.

This preservation of the realm of poetry as a world in itself
is further stressed by the upholding of the fiction that the poet
is still living in that conventionally accepted 'poetical' age of
simplicity, when the utensils of his craft were tablets and the
stylus, and his dress the singing robes of the rhapsode. Thus
George in an early poem writes of himself, as the poet: 'Er hat
den griffel der sich sträubt zu führen' ('He has to use the stylus
which resists'), therein signalizing another aspect of the composition of poetry, as conceived by him and those who have
shared his views: namely the difficulty which the poet himself
experiences in composition. Even in the very late poems, in which
contemporary civilization is being criticized and condemned,
the poet has about him the atmosphere of the *vates*, and it is
more natural to think of him in a flowing robe than wearing a
frock coat and a knotted tie. The same fiction of the poet
living in the primitive days of poetry is to be found in the works
of George's French contemporaries, for instance in those of
Henri de Régnier, some of which George translated. Thus in
L'Accueil the poet makes use of a 'calame de roseau, Dont la
pointe subtile aide à fixer le mot, Sur la tablette lisse et couverte
de cire'. And though his clothes are ragged, when his visitors
expect him to be 'drapé de pourpre hautaine', it is in 'une robe
de laine, Qui se troue à l'épaule et se déchire au bras' that he is
dressed, and by no means in knickerbockers and Norfolk
jacket.

In spite of George's insistence upon comprehensibility
together with precision of line as an essential element in a poem,
he did not meet his readers more than halfway. Apart from the
use of recondite words, he added to the difficulty of an immediate

apprehension of his meaning by devices of printing, such as the absence of capital letters where the German usage expects them, and the reduction of the signs of punctuation (in that over-punctuated language) to a minimum. It would of course be absurd to suggest that these devices were intended to make his poems more difficult to understand. The aim was primarily an aesthetic one, connected with the appearance of the printed page. To all questions of typography, the fount used, the disposition of the print upon the page, the decoration of the binding and pages, he gave detailed personal attention. Gothic type as well as gothic script he abhorred, and *Die Blätter für die Kunst* contains the statement that Germany cannot expect to become a civilized country whilst it retains a barbarous type of print. As far as the reduction of the marks of punctuation is concerned, the disappearance in particular of commas from the pages of his works was not merely in the interest of the appearance of the page, but was also due to his opinion that the grammatical division of sentences which the comma marks conflicted with the poetical rhythm, which calls for other pauses. Underlying this last consideration is George's idea that poetry should be spoken rather than read from the page. He had his own mode of reading, which was a slow solemn declamation based upon the intoning of the office in the Catholic church.

To these surface difficulties to the understanding of George's poetry—the deeper ones are no more than those to which every serious poet may legitimately lay claim as his right—may be added (at any rate for readers outside Germany) the concentrated and compact use of language, whereby he avoids, as far as possible, the little connecting colourless words—prepositions, articles and conjunctions. This forces him often to the genitive construction; 'ich forschte bleichen eifers nach dem horte'; or he avoids the preposition by means of present and perfect participles; or prefers such turns of phrase as: 'ich ihrer und sie meiner götter lachten' instead of 'ich lachte über ihre götter und sie lachten über meine'. The elimination of so many of these little connecting words, whilst it produces an effect of compactness, has also the effect of slowing down the movement of the line by the greater tightness of verbal texture.

No doubt the symbolical type of poem presents difficulties which are absent in a poem which is the immediate expression of feeling. The Symbolist poet gives expression to his poetical idea not in the language of direct emotion, but in the presentation of some image of a thing, a person, a situation, which is the symbol of the idea; unless therefore he uses generally accepted symbols, or such as are easily decipherable, he runs the risk of being difficult of comprehension. George writes almost exclusively symbolical poems, and in the earlier volume where the presentation of a 'Stimmung' (*un état d'âme*) is primarily his aim, the basic significance of the poem is easily revealed by the appositeness of the symbol chosen. Thus *Die Spange* at the end of *Pilgerfahrten* and *Vogelschau* at the end of *Algabal*, by their place in the order of poems, hint at once at some significance with regard to the poet's situation. In *Das Jahr der Seele* the poem which begins 'Die blume, die ich mir am fenster hege' sheds its material significance and reveals its emotional message on a first reading; even in the last volume, *Das Neue Reich*, the poem *Das Lied* is manifestly beneath its legendary narrative a statement of the poet's lot on earth. But not all of George's poems yield up their symbolical meaning so readily. It may perhaps be legitimately assumed that such poems have in their composition a more conscious effort of the will, a greater attention to the elements of form and the deliberate choice of words than the poems which are the direct expression of feeling, and such poems as come, so to speak, surging up unhampered from the subconscious—as Goethe's poem *Über allen Gipfeln ist Ruh* would appear to have done if the traditional account of its composition be the true one. But the over-insistence on the song-like element in lyrical poetry is as restrictive as the undue emphasis upon the element of form. The unpremeditatedness of song of the German poets who were unduly influenced by the *Volkslied* at the beginning of the nineteenth century led them to write countless poems which were trite and trivial in content, and had little but their facile tunefulness to recommend them. These were the poems which had determined the conventional standard of German lyrical poetry throughout the century, and they were the touchstone by which George's formed and fashioned art was tested and usually rejected.

From all that has been said it will be apparent that George was a very self-conscious and deliberate poet, in whom the elements of will and intention were manifestly at work in the process of composition. He took upon himself the rôle of poet and in the light of his conception and conviction of what it should be, he played his rôle with conscientiousness and unremitting attention. But it was his very awareness of himself as *il fabbro* which aroused a feeling of hostility to his poetry—strengthened by the recognition of a similar principle in the conduct of his life—a feeling which expressed itself in such disapproving terms as 'mannered', 'artificial' and 'unnatural' by the general public.

Goethe insisted that it was the characteristic of all art that it was *not* nature; and the demand that art should be 'natural' is made only by those who have failed to recognize that essential distinction. As long as the divergencies of art from nature do not obtrude themselves—for they are present in all art—they are tacitly accepted and overlooked. But the artist who, like George, makes it clear that he is fully aware of the distinction and is working in accordance with this awareness, creates a stumbling block which makes his acceptance by the general public difficult and exposes him to resentment and often ridicule. This was the situation in which George found himself during the greater part of his creative life as a poet in regard to all but a small and discriminating body of readers.

V

In the growing uncertainty and questioning of values in the second half of the nineteenth century art became a moral problem which found expression in the writings of various investigators into the nature of society, notably in the works of Tolstoi. In Germany the dramatist and critic Paul Ernst found it necessary to assign to art an ethical function as a means of educating 'das Volk' before he could with a quietened conscience devote himself to literature as a profession. Ten years later in the early writings of Thomas Mann the dubiety of art became one of the main themes. For Stefan George however no such problem arose. But the unquestioned acceptance of aestheticism with him is made possible by the assimilation to it of two essentially ethical ideas, the ideas of dedication (*Weihe*) and discipline (*Zucht*). These are the controlling forces to which all the poetry of George is subject; and they manifestly imply a sense of responsibility in the practice of his art, which may be implicit in many poets but is rarely so explicitly revealed as in George. The first poem in the early *Hymnen* is entitled *Weihe*. Thus the theme is announced from the beginning, and in some of the other early poems its importance is illustrated by references to another element, *Leidenschaft* (passion), which, since it is inimical to the poet's absolute dedication to his art is represented as an invasion of the sanctuary of poetry by the emotions of ordinary life. The expression of *Zucht* in the world of art is crystallized in the idea of form, that is to say in the unremitting effort of the poet to achieve perfection of form. With Paul Ernst the idea of form is screwed up into a sort of moral compulsion and converted into an operative element in the disciplining of man's ethical being. Thomas Mann, however, in the following decade perceives its twofold possibilities, and speaks in *Der Tod in Venedig* not only of its ethical quality—'als Ergebnis und Ausdruck der Zucht' (the outcome and expression of discipline)—but also of its amoral and even immoral potentialities, since it can be applied to subject matter of all kinds and thus legitimatize the poet's occupation with all that falls under the heading of what Mann stigmatizes as 'das Liederliche' (the disreputable). But with George no such doubt and misgivings were associated with the idea of form, nor indeed with poetry as such at all. It was only in the abuse of poetry, whether in a mistaken choice of subject matter or in an inadequate attention to its formal perfection, that he was concerned to effect a reform. It was the idea of a mission which from the beginning coloured his attitude to the practice of poetry, and this mission was to be carried out not merely by the laying down of certain principles with regard to it in the introductory pages of *Die Blätter für die Kunst*, but also in the actual poems which he himself and those who shared his ideals wrote as examples of the new ideal.

No man, however great a genius, is entirely outside the prevailing taste of the period in which he lives, and George reveals the fact that he belongs to the nineties of the last century both in his acceptance of the idea of the autonomy of art and in his particular conception of beauty itself. The reader of today will often, especially when reading the earlier volumes, find himself uneasily reminded of what was considered artistic or beautiful in the nineties, and no longer is so: thus the artistic adornment of the volumes itself, the description of the appearance of Inspiration in the poem *Weihe*, of the Angel in *Der Teppich des Lebens* and much of the attitudinizing and overcolourfulness of *Algabal*.

George's collected works, including five volumes of translations and one of prose sketches, occupy eighteen volumes in the collected edition; but the volumes contain as a rule not more than 150 pages and the manner of printing is generous of space. His earliest poems are dated 1886. He was then a youth of eighteen. His last poems appeared in collected form in the volume entitled *Das Neue Reich* issued in 1928. Extending therefore over a period of forty years the poems offer the opportunity to survey a poetical and indeed spiritual development, and it seems most suitable to treat them chronologically. If the idea of development be accepted it must be with the reservation that no development in the quality of the poems is implied, on the contrary it may be maintained with some justi-

32

fication that the poems of the middle period (*Das Jahr der Seele*, *Der Teppich des Lebens*, and *Der Siebente Ring*) are the height of George's poetic achievement. The poems in the later volumes, notably in *Der Stern des Bundes* and to a considerable extent in *Das Neue Reich*, are markedly different in form and subject matter from the earlier ones; and the change which has taken place in the poetry reflects the change in the spiritual life of the poet himself, so that here in the more conventional sense the word development is apposite. That development reveals George in the earlier stages as a seeker for illumination, for a significance to life; finding it in his middle period, or rather having it revealed to him; and then using that illumination to survey the world of European civilization at the beginning of the century and pass judgment upon it. Given the nature of the subject matter in *Der Stern des Bundes* it is only to be expected that poetry will set aside her more traditional charms and adopt a severer and harsher mode of expression. One does not expect from the prophet Jeremiah the sweetness of voice of the Song of Solomon.

Die Fibel with its immature beginnings being left aside, the first volume in which the determining and permanent literary influences upon George are operative is the one which includes *Hymnen*; *Pilgerfahrten*; *Algabal* (1892), the three parts of which had been published separately before. It may be noted that the tripartite arrangement within the volumes is common to several of the later collections.

The first group, *Hymnen*, are in the manner of the French Symbolists, more markedly so indeed than the poems in any succeeding volume. The poet seeks to give in each of the poems a presentation (*Darstellung*) of a transitory aspect of his inner life (*état d'âme*) by means of symbols which take the form in many of the poems of aspects of landscape—narrowly circumscribed aspects such as of a terrace with vases; a corner of a park with a fountain; a stretch of sea shore. All are evoked and suggested, not carried out in detail; but with a very noticeable and already masterly employment of colour, which continues indeed throughout the early volumes, as does the ability to make skilful use of vowel sounds to produce a musical effect; for instance, the whistling sound of the reeds in 'die hohen rohre im linden winde ihre fahnen schwingen'. The first poem, *Weihe*, represents the inner preparation of the poet for the coming of Inspiration (*die herrin*) which consecrates him to his function as a poet. Inspiration descends; there is in the description perhaps a recollection of Diana descending to kiss the sleeping Endymion on Mount Latmos. The ideas of blessing bestowed

33

upon the poet, of purification and sacred acceptance, heighten the religious sense of the poet's vocation. But together with the idea of the dedication of the poet there is also the suggestion of the disturbing influences from the outside world, which seek to turn him aside from his ideal task. These disturbing elements are envisaged as human love, and throughout this and the following group of poems we have hints of a conflict between these two elements in the being of the poet. But the love of women plays no important rôle in the poetry of George, and where it appears—mainly in the early volumes—it is never presented with enough intensity to make it convincing: the poet turns too easily from feminine allurements to the claims of his pen for the reader to fear that the temptation was very compelling. In *Das Jahr der Seele* a shadowy 'Freundin' accompanies the poet through the park of his soul and imparts some consolation to his bereaved spirit. With her, woman disappears almost entirely from George's poetry except in verses addressed to friends.[1]

The group ends with a poem called *Die Gärten schliessen*; and the next group, *Pilgerfahrten*, is prepared for by the last line: 'Pilger mit der hand am stabe'. The situation is given in the *Aufschrift* to the next group: George as a pilgrim setting forth in his search for illumination. Endowed with his gift of poetry, feeling himself a dedicated being, but disturbed by the allurements of life to which from time to time he yields, he proceeds upon his solitary way; and the remainder of this volume and the two succeeding ones show him seeking and proving, yielding at times to passion, to melancholy and despair, and communicating in symbolical form his inner experiences. *Pilgerfahrten* shows us more of the conflict between the dedicated poet and those emotional disturbances which militate against the carrying out of his sacred function: his fallings away from his high calling through misgiving, world-weariness, through ignoble contact with the life of the crowd. There are poems of admonition to himself; poems in which he conjures up the journeys of his childhood; one in which the meaninglessness of all growth is symbolized in the attitude of a woman as she looks down upon the flowers in her garden:

> Verdrossen wittert sie den stolz der dinge
> Die nur zum blühen aufgesprossen sind.

[1] The poem *Die Fremde* in *Der Teppich des Lebens* might indeed be regarded as symbolizing woman as the intrusive element in the ordered life.

This group contains two well-known poems: *Mühle, lass die arme still,* and the already mentioned *Die Spange.* Both are symbolical, the former more obscurely so than the latter; but in the narrative subject matter—a number of white-robed girls returning from their first communion and drowned by the breaking of the ice on the lake which they are crossing—there seems to be a possibility of two interpretations. It may be said that the surface meaning of the poem—the facts allusively narrated—is not immediately easy to grasp.

One interpretation brings it into connection with the underlying conflict of these early volumes: the conflict between the element of dedication in the poet's life and the hostile forces of the world without. In this respect the white-robed communicants represent clearly the element of dedication; the 'schwarze Knaben', which draw them down into the dark waters of destruction, the forces which are at war with it. Hence it is a mood of misgiving, even despair, which is symbolized. A second interpretation makes the *Stimmung* which is symbolized the poet's sense of insecurity in a universe where the life of man, consciously controlled, is at the mercy of the darker, profounder, irrational and incomprehensible forces. It is perhaps worth noting with what verbal skill the metallic quality of the frozen landscape is suggested.

The second poem, *Die Spange (The Clasp)*, appears at the end of the collection and its symbolical meaning is clear. 'The Clasp' is George's art. Under the form of this image he is saying that he wished to write cool, simple poetry, but that he has not yet acquired the maturity to do it. He will therefore attempt another kind: the richly ornate, highly coloured, exotic type; and these indeed are the characteristics of the poems in the succeeding group, *Algabal*. The change from the one type of poetry to the other is signalized in the poem not only in the verbal statement but in the difference in the use of vowel sounds in the two stanzas; and the frequency and stressing of the full 'o' sounds in the second stanza—there are seven in three lines—makes the effect of a fanfare heralding the appearance of splendour:

> Ich wollte sie aus kühlem eisen
> Und wie ein glatter fester streif ⸗
> Doch war im schacht auf allen gleisen
> So kein metall zum gusse reif.
>
> Nun aber soll sie also sein:
> Wie eine grosse fremde dolde

Geformt aus feuerrotem golde
Und reichem blitzendem gestein.

Algabal reveals an aspect of George's poetry which is con-
fined to this particular volume and owes much to certain tenden-
cies and movements in French poetry in the second half of the
century, namely to that which is usually stigmatized as *Décadentisme* and attributed to Baudelaire, Rimbaud and above all
to Huysmans: an attitude of mind which has its essential source
in the dissatisfaction of the poets of the time with the material-
istic, scientific civilization which the nineteenth century brought
with it. The particular reaction to the civilization of the age
which finds expression in *Décadentisme* is only one of many
others; all of which, however, are basically a rejection of it.
The *Décadents* go further than the Parnassians and Symbolists,
for they reject the life of nature altogether and seek to set up
in its place an artificial life in which they cultivate a mode of
existence which draws its values from artificiality. The extreme
statement of this attitude of mind is to be found in Huysmans,
and receives explicit expression in the following passages from
A Rebours. In a preface written twenty years later the author
describes how the work came into existence. It was to have
been a brief fantasy:

Je me figurais un monsieur Folantin . . . qui a découvert
dans l'artifice un dérivatif au dégoût qui lui inspirent les
tracas de la vie et les mœurs américains de son temps.

In the novel itself the hero Des Esseintes describes nature thus:

Cette sempiternelle radoteuse a maintenant usé la débon-
naire admiration des vrais artistes, et le moment est venu où
il s'agit de la remplacer, autant que faire se pourra par
l'artifice.

These are the ideas which are put into practice by the hero of the
Algabal poems, the Late Roman Emperor Heliogabalus, and
they represent in extreme form the ideas of George—exaggerated,
over-coloured, the idea of artificiality forced almost into a caricature of itself.

In the spiritual pilgrimage of George to which each volume
of poems bears witness, *Algabal* represents the stage in which
artificiality is glorified and a complete abandonment to it is
essayed and tested as a possible solution in the search for a
satisfying mode of life. George, like Huysmans, rejected it,

but in the working out of the problems of his own being in terms of the emperor-priest he created a work of richness of colouring, rhetorical splendour and a certain outmoded beauty. The identification of George with Algabal is of course not complete. It is not so much with the perverse and cruel tyrant, which according to history he was, but with one who was both priest and emperor and thus set aside by his position from the ordinary life of man—in that sense 'dedicated' as George felt himself to be as a poet.

The work is dedicated to the memory of King Ludwig II of Bavaria, the patron of Wagner, the lover of the arts, who sought to realize in concrete form the dreams of his romantic soul, who rejected life as he experienced it in the civilization around him, attempted to create an artificial mode of life of his own and ultimately died by drowning. In the *Aufschrift* George addresses the king as 'a derided martyr king' and speaks of himself as 'his younger brother'.

Algabal is divided into three parts: *Im Untergrund*; *Tage*; *Andenken*. The first describes the emperor's subterranean palace and gardens, and it is in this part that the rejection of nature and the glorification of artificiality appear most clearly. The second part, *Tage*, records incidents and situations in the life of Algabal during the years of his rule. The third, *Andenken*, gives, as its title suggests, his memories and musings upon that period of rule after it is over. Part I has four poems: the first describes in a general way the realm he has created.

Wo ausser dem seinen kein wille schaltet
Und wo er dem licht und dem wetter gebeut.

The second describes the golden room, the third the silver room of his underground palace; the fourth his subterranean garden. Thus he speaks of it:

Mein garten bedarf nicht luft und nicht wärme ⟩
Der garten den ich mir selber erbaut
Und seiner vögel leblose schwärme
Haben noch nie einen frühling geschaut.

Tage gives impressions of the life and of the character of Algabal. In him there is also that duality which appears in different forms in these early poems of George: tender and cruel, beauty-loving and vindictive, a thinker and a voluptuary, asking himself after he has put his subjects to death whether he has really hated them; satisfied with himself that he has killed a

37

pair of lovers sleeping beneath a tree and thus prevented them from waking to a life which would have interrupted the enjoyment of their love; putting a slave to death who had disturbed his doves while he was feeding them, and then causing the slave's name to be inscribed in the golden goblet from which he drank the following evening.

This collection of poems is unlike much of the early works of George in so far as the poet has made a coherent symbol for himself in the person of Algabal and lived through a certain phase of experience in his imagined hero. The same pattern recurs, though less definitely, and with an unnamed hero in *Die Hängenden Gärten*. But this phase of experience is now over—a solution has been tried but has proved inadequate; new experiences must be sought and put to the test. At the end of *Algabal* stands the poem *Vogelschau*—'Weisse schwalben sah ich fliegen' (white swallows I saw flying); it represents a turning away from the exotic, from the world of 'Unnatur', symbolized in underground palaces and gardens, from the artificiality of a realm constructed entirely by the hand of man in defiance of nature. The 'bunte Häher' (gaily coloured jays) of the 'Wald der Tusferi' (wood of Tusferi) of the second stanza; the 'Raben' (ravens) and 'schwarze Dohlen' (black daws) of the third stanza are representative of all that, and we come in the final stanza to the 'weisse Schwalben' again but now no longer 'in dem Winde hell und heiss' (in the bright and burning wind) but 'in dem Winde kalt und klar' (in the cold and clear wind). This poem forms the transition from the atmosphere of the world of Algabal to one in which there prevails a more tonic and astringent air, which gives the atmosphere for the next collection: *Das Buch der Hirten*.

The poems of this collection have as their setting the Greece of the idylls, not the heroic Greece but the every-day pastoral, bucolic life. The second collection, *Das Buch der Sagen und Sänge*, has the Middle Ages for its setting; the third, *Das Buch der Hängenden Gärten*, the Orient. In none of the collections is there any attempt at an archaeological reconstruction of a past age. The civilizations chosen are symbols of states of mind of the poet—stages in his search for illumination of the significance of life. Each one represents an attitude to life, of which the figures which appear in the poems are representatives; and the poems in all these books are concerned with imaginary figures. These may well be projections of the poet's inner life, but each poem considered individually and apart from its setting still remains a self-contained evocation of a person, a mood, a situation, thus carrying out the principle announced in *Die Blätter*

für die Kunst that the aim of poetry was presentation, not reflection, the transformation of the poetical idea into a concrete
form. In no one of the poems appears a character vouched for
by history; but the figures, though imaginary, are nevertheless
typical of a situation or of the period of which they are representative. In this collection appears clearly for the first time the
very marked habit of the later George to present characters,
which interest not so much by their individual qualities as by
their existence as types, so that a certain statue-like quality is
common to most of them.

The contrast between *Algabal*—George's most colourful and
brilliant achievement so far—and *Das Buch der Hirten* could
not be greater. From the violent exoticism of the earlier work
he passes to an atmosphere of cool serenity, and the colours
are correspondingly subdued to pastel shades; from the rejection
of nature and the febrile determination to create an artificial
world, to the acceptance of the ordinary life of nature, and to
the picture of a life lived in accordance with it—in accordance
with nature, that is, as it is moulded by immemorial custom and
manifests itself in the communal life of man, unchallenged by
the arbitrariness of the will of the individual. Here are no
passions at work, but a calm following of that which seems to
be the natural order of man's life, though the presentation is
tinged by a certain melancholy, which is indeed apparent in all
the early volumes: the sisters who on the anniversary of the
death of their bridegrooms recall their loss; the shepherd
who set forth for the day in charge of his sheep; the wrestler
who is unaware of the fame which his skill has brought him; the
youths who have been brought up to be servants in the temple
but are not chosen for that office; the first born who must wander
forth from their homes to seek a living elsewhere. All these
figures accept their fate unquestioningly, and of their acceptance a feeling of serenity is begotten, which is deepened by the
poetic treatment itself: the measured, moderate statement, the
coolness of presentation. Nothing here excites or distresses
intensely—everything has the calm and simplicity of figures on
a frieze: the music of the verse is very subdued and solemnly
moving; its metrical form the long unrhymed line.

The periods chosen in these collections are, as has been said,
symbols of states of mind of the poet. Thus though they are
successively investigated and presented, they exist also con-
temporaneously. In turning away from bucolic Greece, George
is not rejecting it as he had rejected the world of Algabal.
No single period symbolizes his whole ideal of life; it is in the
combination of the three that this consists.

It has been said that George's ideal of life lies in the synthesis of the three elements of which man is compounded: 'Geist, Seele und Leib' (spirit, soul and body); though in his later works more importance is assigned to 'Leib'. The terms as used by George defy an exact definition but it may roughly be said that 'Geist' represents the living in accordance with ones destiny; 'Seele' the elements of enthusiasm, devotion and loyalty; 'Leib' the recognition of the body and the sensuous life. In passing from *Das Buch der Hirten* to *Das Buch der Sagen und Sänge* we find ourselves again in a world—the world of the Middle Ages—which seemed to George at this time to have produced a harmonized and unified life, just as the Greece of the earlier collection had done, but of a different kind. Again we have poems presenting characteristic figures of a period—for George it is largely the period of chivalry and song, with religious devotion as an integral element of it. Thus: the youth keeping watch before the altar on the eve of his being dubbed a knight (*Sporen-wache*); the companions in arms; the hermit; the knight and his lady parting at dawn; the group of knights-errant in search of the grail; the knight who sleeps when he should be watching; poems suggested by the 'Minnedienst' of the twelfth century; a hymn in praise of the Virgin—all motifs taken from the civilization of the Middle Ages. Again there is no attempt at antiquarian resuscitation of a past age. George lets his imagination wander through mediaeval times and identifies aspects of his own inner life with certain figures, certain characteristic situations. The theme of dedication and passion in conflict recurs once or twice: in *Der Ritter der sich verschlief*, and more markedly in *Sporenwache*, in which for a moment the youth forgets his religious dedication during the vigil and the picture of a maiden he had once seen passes before his thoughts.

The beautiful youth in heroic pose or in heroic function is one of the characteristic figures which appears in all these early collections. It is central with George, for it is the symbol at this stage of 'das schöne Leben'; it occurs again in *Der Teppich des Lebens* and ultimately transcends even the symbolical and becomes the realization of 'das schöne Leben' in the ideal figure of Maximin in *Der Siebente Ring* and *Der Stern des Bundes*.

The poems of the next collection: *Die Hängenden Gärten*[1] are more akin to the poems of *Algabal*, though without their violence and cult of artificiality. After the bucolic world of the shepherds and the heroic world of the Middle Ages, the world of this oriental ruler is assayed as a symbol of the sensuous life.

[1] Schoenberg set fifteen of these poems to music in 1906.

Thus after the life of the spirit and the life of soul, the life of the body is examined as a possible mode from which satisfaction may be obtained. As in *Algabal* a certain vague succession of events, hinted at rather than stated, forms the string upon which the poems are threaded, so in this collection there is a central figure, though he is not named. Ruler and priest, he neglects his functions as such for love; half of his country is overrun by the enemy; he goes as a minstrel slave to the court of another ruler; gives this up, too, from an inner dissatisfaction and a sense of the valuelessness of all activity. In the last poem but one, he is seen looking back upon all he has lost. He hears voices from the stream—the last poem, *Stimmen im Strome*,—which call to him and promise him recovery, refuge and peace. But even this may not bring satisfaction. Beyond it is annihilation, dissolution, absorption into the elements. This poem with its floating, swaying music (largely due to the frequent use of present participles) represents this in symbolical form in the voices of the water nymphs who draw him down to the pleasures of their life beneath the waves, promising him ultimate bliss in his dissolution and transformation into the waves themselves.

In so far as the three worlds represented in the three books are spirit, soul and body, at the end of the third book the synthesis of the three has not been achieved, though no one of the three has been rejected. It is no doubt logical that the end of the book which is symbolical of 'Leib' should be dissolution, since that is the end of the body and all that pertains thereto. A comparison between the last poems in each of the three collections reveals a positive note only in the second one, which represents 'Seele' in the hymn to the Virgin *Lilie der Aue*. The last poem in *Das Buch der Hirten* is called *Das Ende des Siegers* and suggests that the hero in the last resort will be overcome. Wounded by the monster which escapes him, with a wound that will not heal, he ends in pitiable decay. It would seem therefore that in so far as no synthesis has yet been brought about between the claims of spirit, soul and body, the most positive and enduring value is that offered by 'Seele'. The conflict 'Weihe–Leidenschaft' which appears in the earlier collections fades out with *Das Buch der Hängenden Gärten*.

The next volume establishes a connection with the earlier ones by its very title. The poet still upon his 'Pilgerfahrten', after essaying all these modes of experience, having rejected some and turned aside from the exclusive acceptance of any, turns back to his own soul and holds communion with himself in the park-like landscape of *Das Jahr der Seele*. The settings of the earlier collection had been drawn from the historical past or the exotic or the artificially imaginative. Here the background is nature, but nature moulded and controlled by the hand of man and almost in its particular form created by it. The background is to a great extent revealed by suggestion rather than by direct description; but with the colours, the atmosphere, the feel of Autumn, Winter and Summer as much conditioning the 'Stimmungen' of the 'ich' and 'du' of the poems as conditioned by them. What belongs to nature exclusively and is not the effect of the hand of man is primarily the ordered procession of the seasons, and even from this Spring has been omitted.

The volume entitled *Das Jahr der Seele*[1] falls again into three parts, of which the first is the one covered by the title; the second part is devoted to poems concerned with personal friends; the third is called *Traurige Tänze*. The first part has a further tripartite division: *Nach der Lese (Autumn)*, *Waller im Schnee (Winter)* and *Sieg des Sommers*. In all of them the atmosphere of the particular season is sensitively caught and expressed.

In a preface warning the readers not to try and identify places or characters George wrote: 'Seldom are 'ich' and 'du' so much the same soul as in this book'. With this indication from George it seems justifiable to assume that they represent the soul of the poet communing with itself. The first part of the book suggests a point of repose, of self-collection after the experiences recorded in the works already passed under review; is it perhaps in nature after all that the illumination will be found? But there seems a weariness, a sense of the fruitlessness of his quest, there is no Spring in the year of his soul, and a certain melancholy hangs over the whole giving it a music of its own. There is almost a renunciation of hope and the acceptance of a second-best until the real illumination, now almost despaired of, makes its appearance. Throughout the work the fiction of a 'du', of the presence of a second person, is maintained; and this 'du' is a gracious visitor, who understands and soothes the distress of one who is seeking direction in life and awaiting illumination. The suggestion, at least, that the companion (a woman) is not the Beloved herself but one who must be accepted in her place, is given in poems two and three. But the atmosphere of the whole work is tentative, vaguely expectant, and indeed the Angel, who is to bring the illumination in *Der Teppich des Lebens*, is prefigured in the lines:

> Drüben an dem strand ein bruder
> Winkt das frohe banner schwenkend.

---

[1] Schoenberg set one poem from this volume to music; Webern also one for mixed chorus *a capella*.

But all is symbolical—the 'ich' and the 'du', the seasons of the year; and the park in which the lovers walk is the soul of the poet.

The poems are all written in four-lined stanzas and with few exceptions in eleven syllabled lines, so that throughout the work feminine rhymes predominate. It is no doubt partly this which gives to this collection a musical quality which has made it the most popular and the most quoted form of George's works. It is not even necessary to perceive the symbolic meaning in order to realize that here are poems which will bear comparison in purely poetic quality, even in the most conventional acceptance of the term, with favourite anthology pieces in German literature.

> Umkreisen wir den stillen teich
> In den die wasserwege münden!
> Du suchst mich heiter zu ergründen
> Ein wind umweht uns frühlings-weich.
>
> Die blätter die den boden gilben
> Verbreiten neuen wolgeruch ⁄
> Du sprichst mir nach in klugen silben
> Was mich erfreut im bunten buch.
>
> Doch weisst du auch vom tiefen glücke
> Und schätzest du die stumme träne?
> Das auge schattend auf der brücke
> Verfolgest du den zug der schwäne.

Doubtless this poem is symbolical, though its symbolical significance is not apparent on the surface, deeper than which the ingenuous reader need not penetrate in order to perceive its poetical beauty, and this fact makes its acceptance more easy. The same may be said also of the poem in *Waller im Schnee*:

> Die blume die ich mir am fenster hege
> Verwahrt vorm froste in der grauen scherbe
> Betrübt mich nur trotz meiner guten pflege
> Und hängt das haupt als ob sie langsam sterbe
>
> Um ihrer frühern blühenden geschicke
> Erinnerung aus meinem sinn zu merzen
> Erwähl ich scharfe waffen und ich knicke
> Die blasse blume mit dem kranken herzen.

Was soll sie nur zur bitternis mir taugen?
Ich wünschte dass vom fenster sie verschwände ...
Nun heb ich wieder meine leeren augen
Und in die leere nacht die leeren hände.

Like the former poem it can be appreciated without its symbolic
reference which, however, is here more easily recognized: the
sickly flower, the poet's decision to cut it, the sense of emptiness
which is the result of his action—all this refers to some inward
circumstances, such as the deliberate crushing of a hope, an
ambition, a love.

The second part of the volume consists of poems addressed to
George's personal friends, and circumstances connected with
their reunions. Part of their significance is inevitably lost to
those readers who are unacquainted either with the friends or
with the circumstances, but there are some poems among them
concerned with George's own inner life and situation at this
time which are illuminating in that respect. The third part of the
collection, *Traurige Tänze*, moves back again into an atmosphere
tinged with the melancholy of the poems of *Das Jahr der Seele*.
Like these they are all in four-lined stanzas, but here each poem
consists of three stanzas. The length of line has a greater variety
than in those of the earlier groups. Some—*Dies leid und diese
last* for instance—are lyrics of weariness and despair. This
weariness is lightened in some of the poems by the determination
to make the best of what is available, to be thankful for what *is*,
since the great illumination has not come; to welcome autumn
because there has been no spring. The mood sways up and
down, from poem to poem. If they are dances they are sad
dances. As in *Das Jahr der Seele* there is the assumption of a
companionship of 'ich' and 'du' and many of the poems are
addressed to the 'du'. The following poem gives the prevailing
mood of the whole group: acceptance of and gratitude for what is,
with a sense that it is a second best, that something has been missed
which would have solved all problems and realized all aspirations:

Es lacht in dem steigenden jahr dir
Der duft aus dem garten noch leis.
Flicht in dem flatternden haar dir
Eppich und ehrenpreis.

Die wehende saat ist wie gold noch ⁄
Vielleicht nicht so hoch mehr und reich ⁄
Rosen begrüssen dich hold noch ⁄
Ward auch ihr glanz etwas bleich.

Verschweigen wir was uns verwehrt ist ⁄
Geloben wir glücklich zu sein
Wenn auch nicht mehr uns beschert ist
Als noch ein rundgang zu zwein.

But throughout the prevailing melancholy of these poems there is a sense of expectancy; and the coming of illumination which is heralded in the last poem of *Waller im Schnee* by the appearance of the brother on the shore who 'beckons, waving his joyous banner' is repeated in the lines:

Mein feuchtes auge späht nur fern
Nach diesem Einen aus der gern
Die harfe reich und wohlgestimmt
Der unsre goldne harfe nimmt ⁄

Nor is there absent an element which varies the dominating tone of melancholy: the note of admonition or self-encouragement—for as in *Das Jahr der Seele*, the 'ich' and 'du' must ultimately be considered parts of the poet's own soul. Thus one poem concludes with the lines:

Nicht vor der eisigen firnen
Drohendem rätsel erschrick
Und zu den ernsten gestirnen
Hebe den suchenden blick!

And there are other poems in which the same note is struck.

VI

The tendency to see George as a figure of masterfulness, of complete self-possession, to which the later volumes lend some evidence has been extended to cover the whole of his life. This is a simplification of his personality which is not justified. Up to and including *Das Jahr der Seele* there is a continuous reference in the poems to states of mind which are far from indicating such a convinced attitude of self-possession. As has been suggested, all these earlier collections express a seeking and proving of possible modes of life, and in all of them there are poems which are the expressions of uncertainty, misgiving, doubt and even of world-weariness and despair, so that on the whole it may be said that a sense of melancholy prevails, not least in *Das Jahr der Seele* and in *Traurige Tänze*. It is only from *Der*

Teppich des Lebens onwards that the personality of George, as revealed in his poetry, presents the appearance under which he is generally envisaged, and emerges as that of one whose attitude to life is a positive one: masterful, autocratic, even dictatorial.

For the poems included in *Der Teppich des Lebens* (1899), above all in the poems of the *Vorspiel*, announce the illumination, the promise of fulfilment, the attainment of which had been the aspiration recorded in all the earlier poems. The *Vorspiel* is also in a more inward sense a prelude—a prelude to the revelation of Maximin, which forms the core of the following volume: *Der Siebente Ring. Der Teppich des Lebens* has again a tripartite division; *Vorspiel*; *Teppich des Lebens*; *Lieder von Traum und Tod*. With this volume a new idea enters George's poetry —the idea of a *message*. The idea of a *mission* had been implicit in his poetry from the beginning; now it becomes more explicit, fortified by the message. In the *Vorspiel*, it is as yet a message delivered to him by the Angel; but in the later volumes it will become a message which he himself is called to deliver to his country and his generation. In the twenty-four poems which make up the *Vorspiel* the ideal of life which is to be his is announced by the Angel to him, and the various tentative modes represented in the earlier volumes coalesce and are crystallized in the ideal of 'das schöne leben', which is henceforth to determine his thinking.

The first poem describes the appearance of the Angel to the almost despairing poet: he comes as the messenger of 'das schöne leben', and it is noteworthy that his voice is almost identical with that of the poet— 'und seine stimme fast der meinen glich' from which it is to be assumed that here again— as in *Das Jahr der Seele*—there is an externalization of a part of George's own inner life, the part that has now found an adjustment to the claims of spirit, soul and body, in which adjustment 'das schöne leben' is realized, and the manifestation of 'das schöne leben' is the body. In the successive poems—all poems of equal length (four quatrains of solemn and sustained movement) the Angel announces and the poet accepts a certain mode of life. He will live in solitude, at the most only among a few chosen companions all of whom share his ideals with him. The course of his life will now be altered: no longer will he journey to foreign lands; the landscape of his native land, the landscape of the Rhine will be his chosen province, from which he will speak to his own people.

It is at this point that George takes up the rôle of the *German* poet; and though this is often held against him, the charge seems hardly a legitimate one. His assumption of this rôle contains no chauvinistic elements; and if he assumes it half way through his career, it must be remembered that most other German poets, Hölderlin, for instance, were such from the beginning, and it is odd to find fault with a poet for being primarily the poet of his own country. Moreover his Germanism is so shot through with Greek elements that he might have said with Hölderlin: 'The Greeks are indispensable to us'. Indispensable because in his view (as in Hölderlin's) Germans could only realize themselves as Germans by assimilating the ideal life of Greece to their lives. In the seventh poem, the Angel lays down for the poet the course he is to pursue: turning aside from all controversy even with the sages, contemplating life from a point of vantage, assessing the value of things but taking no care to acquire them; following not Christianity but the spirit of Greece—'Hellas ewig unsre liebe'.

The poet has descended now from his ivory tower to the street. 'Du stiegest ab von deinem hohen hause zum wege.' There he will still remain, a stranger from a distant shore to the multitude whom he has hitherto avoided. They cannot understand him; but now and again a kindred spirit will comprehend his ideals and a community will be established:

> Nur manchmal bricht aus ihnen edles feuer
> Und offenbart dir dass ihr bund nicht schände.
> Dann sprich: in starker schmerzgemeinschaft euer
> Erfass ich eure brüderlichen hände.

Already in these poems of the *Vorspiel* appears the prophetic idea of a new community of race and people. The poet is to take up his place among those leaders and rulers in the world of the spirit whose influence has spread over centuries. He feels his mission as a leader in that world confirmed; and he conceives of history as the sum of these great and heroic personalities—of whom he himself is one—who are the vital factors in the development of mankind. The *Vorspiel* is the central manifesto of George's doctrine of life.

The actual *Teppich des Lebens* forms the second part of the collection and is introduced by the poem *Der Teppich* (*The Tapestry*). This explains the title of the volume. The poems are to give pictures of characteristic figures which make up the pattern of life, illuminate aspects of it and declare its significance. They are individual figures, but all presented with a simplicity, abstractness and sometimes allusiveness which make them rather types and symbols than differentiated individuals, and with a general tendency to see them heroically as figures taken from a primitive form of life. All the poems are in the same form as those of the *Vorspiel*. They include such poems as *Urlandschaft*—a picture of a primaeval landscape into which man makes his irruption; *Der Freund der Fluren*—the gardener tending his plants; *Der Jünger*—the disciple; *Die Fremde*—the strange woman who comes to the village, creates disturbance there by her allurements, and disappears leaving behind only the child which she has borne there. Characteristic figures are represented already in *Das Buch der Hirten* and *Das Buch der Sagen und Sänge* with their settings of antiquity or the Middle Ages. George's method here is not new to him, but it has received confirmation from the message of the Angel. It continues throughout the later volumes. Such poems may be described, making use of George's own title for a number of poems in this collection, as *Standbilder—Standbilder der Menschheit* (*Statues of the human race*); heroically seen, sometimes presenting in rather abstract fashion typical aspects of life, and calculated to stimulate a sense of human greatness and pride, though not all represent admirable aspects of human life.

The next volume, *Der Siebente Ring*[1], which did not appear until eight years later, is considerably larger than any of the others and is of primary importance, for it embodies the ideas enunciated in the *Vorspiel* of *Der Teppich des Lebens*, embodies in fact in the person of Maximin 'das schöne leben', whose messenger had visited George in the earlier volume. It is divided into seven parts, and the fourth, the central one, entitled *Maximin*, is the core of the work, anticipated in the first three parts, and reflected upon those that follow it. It is in this volume that George appears not only as the poet with a message, but also as the seer; and thus the thought content of his poems acquires increasing importance. George himself in the opening poem entitled *Das Zeitgedicht* anticipates the surprise which his contemporaries will feel when faced with the change in his poetry and in the poet himself; that he whom they formerly blamed for his aesthetic withdrawal from life (whilst they themselves rushed into it with uproar and hideous greed); he whose inner struggles and torments they had failed to recognize —that he should have exchanged his pipings for the brazen notes of the trumpet. Where they see change however there is in reality continuation, for it may be that all beauty, strength and greatness will arise tomorrow from the calm flutings of a youth.

Zeitgedichte are poems which attack contemporary social and

---

[1] Schoenberg set two poems from this volume to music, Webern five.

political abuses and prevailing attitudes of mind which are felt to be evil. They are nothing new in German literature. In Heine's second collection of poems one division bears this title. But Heine's *Zeitgedichte* are more direct in their attack and often more scurrilous; those of George are basically concerned with heroic judgments passed on the actual conditions of civilization. In a second poem bearing the same title *Das Zeitgedicht* describes itself as the voice of conscience, disturbing the complacency of the contemporary world. George, unlike Heine, uses the symbolic method of presentation which he has maintained throughout: pictures of the heroic past such as the Porta Nigra of Trier; the tombs of ancient German kings at Speier; or heroic and distinguished personalities such as Dante; Nietzsche; Leo XIII; Boecklin; all these serve to stress by contrast the degeneracy of the present age and of the masses. This part of the volume, however, and the following one (*Gestalten*) stand somewhat apart from the poems which form the core of the book: the third, fourth, fifth and sixth parts— *Gezeiten* (*Tides*); *Maximin*; *Traumdunkel* and *Lieder*. In these is celebrated the achievement, the manifestation of 'das schöne Leben' in the person of Maximin, the beautiful, gifted youth who is deified by George.

It is this deification of Maximin that constitutes the stumbling block for many an appreciative reader of George's poetry; and indeed the various subtle and metaphysical interpretations of the poet's cult of Maximin, offered by disciples, seem almost calculated to make things worse. For Maximin emerges not merely as a symbol of the godhead, but as the god himself:

> Dem bist du kind ∕ dem freund.
> Ich seh in dir den Gott
> Den schauernd ich erkannt
> Dem meine andacht gilt.

The nearest approach to this relationship in literature is that of Dante to Beatrice: but Beatrice is the symbol of Divine Truth, not Divine Truth itself. In Maximin, in his presence as long as he lives, in the cult of him after his death (a certain parallel may be seen in Novalis's cult of the dead Sophie) George finds the god incarnate, as well as the realization of 'das schöne Leben' which the Angel had announced to him. In him the deity is embodied, and the body deified. George met Maximin only a year or two before the boy's death, and he remained ever after the centre of a quasi-religious, quasi-mystical experience. This adoration is prefigured in earlier writings of

49

George, above all in the idea that nothing really exists except in so far as it is 'gestaltet', receives form. From this hypostasis of form there is perhaps only a step to the belief that the godhead must manifest itself in the perfect body, indeed that the perfect body *is* the godhead.

A statement in a later number of *Die Blätter für die Kunst* (1910) will elucidate, even if it does not make acceptable, this conception of the divine, attributed by the writer to the Greeks:

> . . . of all the utterances of the thousands of years which are known to us, the Greek idea that the body is god—the body which is the symbol of transitoriness—was by far the most creative, . . . by far the boldest and the most worthy of mankind, and surpasses in sublimity every other, including the Christian one.

(The words 'der leib sei der gott'—are printed in large capitals.) But whatever attitude may be taken to this experience of George's, it is nevertheless clear that in this transformation of a human being into a divinity George's seeking and striving for significance in life found its fulfilment. Indeed it was prepared by his exclusive concern with the education of male youth and the continually recurring figure of the beautiful young hero in the earlier poems. Thus there is a certain logic in the Maximin climax to George's life. The figure of Maximin dominates the whole of *Der Siebente Ring*, but there can be no doubt that the poems which celebrate the more human relationship of the master to the disciple, the delight in his presence, the intensity of affection he evokes, the poignancy of grief felt at his death are more impressive poetically, have a more spontaneous movement and possess a greater warmth than those poems which are concerned with the deification of the boy. In the poems celebrating the purely human relationship it would seem that the spirit of love—and it was its only full flowering in George's life—has broken down barriers and released constraints of expression which are clearly felt in other parts of George's *œuvre*. In the division *Gezeiten*, in which the human intercourse between George and Maximin finds expression, George's poetic quality is at its finest, and some of this quality flows over into the songs in the latter part of the volume, awakening sympathy and tenderness for a grief which was manifestly so deeply and poignantly felt. But this has reference primarily to Maximin the human being; with Maximin the god, the attempt is made to surround him with all the attendant circumstance of a godhead who triumphs over death and remains a living being in the minds of his worshippers. And the reader remains fundamentally unmoved. It is unlikely that many, outside of George's own circle, will feel able to accept Maximin as a religious revelation, even though they may accept him as a poetic inspiration. They may rather regard all the religious paraphernalia as a sign of the urgent need of George's generation to find a substitute for the gods who had disappeared. This, it seems, is the only explanation for the strange fact that a youth of sixteen years, unknown and unobserved until George observed him, endowed with whatever beauty and gifts of personality, should be found suitable to support divinity and should be divinely proclaimed by so selective a spirit as George, and as a god imposed upon his followers. But the figure of Maximin thus conceived becomes for George a centre of light and a symbol of perfection; and by the standard of this symbol George tested and indignantly rejected contemporary life. In the last volumes of his poetry he judges, reproves, warns, admonishes and foresees imminent destruction. Thus in *Der Stern des Bundes* (1914) and *Das Neue Reich* (1928), the last two volumes, the spirit of the *Zeitgedichte* and the spirit of the Maximin poems combine to form a unity of inspiration.

In the poems of *Der Stern des Bundes* it is the voice of the poet-seer, poet-prophet which prevails. Where in the *Zeitgedichte* the evils of contemporary civilization are denounced implicitly by reference to figures who stand in contrast to it, in the later volume the attack is more direct. Raising his voice as the seer, George warns against the degeneracy of modern times, castigates the weaknesses and falseness of democracy, refutes the belief in a fallacious prosperity, pours scorn upon materialism and the falsely optimistic idea of progress based upon it, deplores the absence of heroism, and foresees still greater evils to come. It is the voice of one crying in the wilderness that the day of judgment is at hand. The message continues to be expressed in abstract, symbolic terms—no reference is made to concrete instances, no names are mentioned to be held up to obloquy, no place is named. Often the setting seems to be suggested by classical themes or borrowed from the Bible. Through this world of symbols the figure of George passes, proclaiming the wrath to come, the destruction which is now inevitable. In one poem he contrasts the present with past times, scorning the belief of the present generation that their times show greater freedom and tolerance than the Dark Ages. These at least had a god on whose behalf cruel things were done, but modern times have set up an idol in his place and into its jaws they hurl their best. In another he cites, without naming him, Nietzsche as the last warner, the last to show the possibility of salvation. But the people paid no heed: they continued to talk, to laugh, to mock. The warner departed— now it is too late, no arm now will hold up the spokes of the wheel which is rolling down into the void.

Der Stern des Bundes is a very homogeneous work, consisting of short poems each of a dozen lines or so, mainly unrhymed. It has a division called *Eingang*, followed by three books. The spirit of which Maximin is the embodiment broods over the whole. In the *Eingang* there are poems which suggest a communion between the poet and the dead youth, who strengthens and confirms him in his task. The first book contains the poems as already described, hortatory, denunciatory, menacing. The second book, like the *Eingang*, is concerned with Maximin and, recalling the days of their earthly friendship, asserts a communion with him after his death. The third book contains poems of admonition, which seem to be addressed not to a wider public but rather to a chosen circle of initiates. And indeed in a prefatory note attached to the public version George explains that the book was intended originally for the friends of his inner circle; but that appearing as it did immediately before the outbreak of war in 1914 it was interpreted as a breviary for the men on the battlefields. This however was not his intention: 'The events of 1914 made the minds of a wider public receptive for a book which might have remained a secret book for years'. A certain quasi-mystical note is present in these poems which is new in George. For instance, the poem which begins:

> Ich bin der Eine und bin Beide
> Ich bin der zeuger bin der schoss
> Ich bin der degen und die scheide
> Ich bin das opfer bin der stoss.

It is only too easy to see how the words of the final chorus could be interpreted as referring to the war upon which young Germans were setting out, and how readily a nationalistic meaning could be attached to them:

> Gottes pfad ist uns geweitet
> Gottes land ist uns bestimmt
> Gottes krieg ist uns entzündet
> Gottes kranz ist uns erkannt.

But it was in intention for a smaller community and a different campaign that the chorus was written.

The poems are frequently difficult and obscure. Considered as pure poetry there is little to charm in them and though they may represent the summit of George's thought, they do not represent the summit of his poetical achievement. One—symbolical, but easily comprehensible in its symbolism—may stand as a representative of many.

> Wer je die flamme umschritt
> Bleibe der flamme trabant!
> Wie er auch wandert und kreist:
> Wo noch ihr schein ihn erreicht
> Irrt er zu weit nicht vom ziel.
> Nur wenn sein blick sie verlor
> Eigener schimmer ihn trügt:
> Fehlt ihm der mitte gesetz
> Treibt er zerstiebend ins all

The last book which George published, *Das neue Reich* (1928), contains poems written during the 1914-18 war and in the years of anarchy in Germany which followed it. Let it not be assumed that it is a glorification of any new political realm: indeed, it would seem rather from the tone of the poems that the realm is visionary. Many of the poems have reference to the war and some appeared separately before 1918. On the whole it is the voice of the poet-seer which speaks, especially in the first section—the voice of one who has seen his warnings of calamity realized in the event; who has been present at the destruction of the civilization whose end he had foretold. If his judgement of the state of affairs seems harsh and rigid it is because he will not allow a sentimental optimism to blind his vision of truth, nor comforting catch-phrases to lull his ears to the acceptance of a false security; because he will not cry Peace, Peace, when there is no peace. In the symbolical poem *Der Brand des Tempels* he declares that it will be half a thousand years before the temple can be restored. His attitude to the war in the poems dealing with it, more especially in *Der Krieg*, cannot have endeared him to those whose patriotism was of a chauvinistic kind. To those who come to the Seer in their distress and wonder at his calm he replies that he has shed his tears in advance and now has none to shed ... What is to him the murder of hundred thousands, compared to the murder of life itself? He cannot grow excited about native virtue and French treachery ... There is no occasion for rejoicing. There will be no triumph, only the unworthy downfall of many ... Sick worlds pass in fever to their end amidst the tumult. And to those who ask whether he fails to recognize the measure of sacrifice and the strength of the communal spirit, he replies that these things are to be found also on the side of the enemy. At the end of the poem a more conciliatory attitude is taken up by the Seer who, basing his faith upon the youth of his nation, refuses to believe that his country, too beautiful to be laid waste by foreign feet, can perish.

But George speaks in these poems not exclusively as the prophet whose warning words have been ignored and are now fulfilled in the destruction around him. In the poem *Hyperion* he sees himself also as the prophet of a newer and better civilization which he as a dying man will not live to see:

> Mein leidend leben neigt dem schlummer zu
> Doch gütig lohnt der Himmlischen verheissung
> Dem frommen . . . der im Reich nie wandeln darf;
> Ich werde heldengrab ∕ ich werde scholle
> Der heilige sprossen zur vollendung nahn:
> MIT DIESEM KOMMT DAS ZWEITE ALTER ∕ LIEBE
> GEBAR DIE WELT ∕ LIEBE GEBIERT SIE NEU.
> Ich sprach den spruch ∕ der zirkel ist gezogen . . .
> Eh mich das dunkel überholt entrückt
> Mich hohe schau: bald geht mit leichten sohlen
> Durch teure flur greifbar im glanz der Gott.

It was certainly not Hitler whom George foresaw as the god who should make all things new.

Another poem, *Der Mensch und der Drud*, reveals a change, of which there are occasional signs in the late volumes, in George's attitude to nature. The hostile attitude to the primaeval aspect of nature has yielded to a recognition, perhaps intellectual rather than emotional, of nature as the basis and indispensable element in human life and of the necessity that humanity should remain in immediate contact with it. In this poem he warns against an excessive intellectualism which is losing touch with the primitive simplicities and instincts of life, from which alone man can draw the strength necessary to sustain existence. Presented in symbolical form as *Der Drud*, or Satyr, these fundamentals of all existence admonish mankind:

> Mit allen künsten lernt ihr nie was euch
> Am meisten frommt . . . wir aber dienen still.
> So hör nur dies: uns tilgend tilgt ihr euch.
> Wo unsre zotte streift nur da kommt milch
> Wo unser huf nicht hintritt wächst kein halm.
> Wär nur dein geist am werk gewesen: längst

Wär euer schlag zerstört und all sein tun
Wär euer holz verdorrt und saatfeld brach. .
Nur durch den zauber bleibt das leben wach.

The last part of the volume is headed *Das Lied* and to it the distich is prefixed:

Was ich noch sinne und was ich noch füge
Was ich noch liebe trägt die gleichen züge.

It is therefore to be expected that the songs which make up this part of the volume will reveal the same qualities as those in the earlier volumes. In point of fact there seems to be in some of these songs of George's old age a freer movement, a greater simplicity and an approximation to what is normally met with in the German *Lieder* of the more traditional poets. Certainly there is no diminution, but rather an increase of the lyric note in such poems as *Das Lied*; *Seelied*; *Das Licht* and the last one of all: *Du schlank und rein wie eine flamme*. *Das Lied* tells in narrative form of the man who went out in his youth to an enchanted country, and found, when he returned, that years had passed, that no one knew him any longer. All thought him mad and set him to tend the flocks. Only the children listened to a song he sang, and still sang it themselves together when he was dead. A subject matter frequent enough in folk legend, here it is clearly a symbolical account of the fate of the poet at the hands of the community. In *Seelied* the old man sitting on the sea shore describes his waiting all day for the child with golden hair, whose coming is the only joy left him. This poem would seem to refer to Maximin. The last poem in the volume is manifestly an evocation of him, of all he had meant to George, of inspiration, beauty, truth, fulfilment of life. It is poetically one of the loveliest poems which George wrote and it stands at the end of his poetical career, a tribute to that which had given meaning and value to his life.

Du schlank und rein wie eine flamme
Du wie der morgen zart und licht
Du blühend reis vom edlen stamme
Du wie ein quell geheim und schlicht

Begleitest mich auf sonnigen matten
Umschauerst mich im abendrauch
Erleuchtest meinen weg im schatten
Du kühler wind du heisser hauch

Du bist mein wunsch und mein gedanke
Ich atme dich mit jeder luft
Ich schlürfe dich mit jedem tranke
Ich küsse dich mit jedem duft

Du blühend reis vom edlen stamme
Du wie ein quell geheim und schlicht
Du schlank und rein wie eine flamme
Du wie der morgen zart und licht.

VII

George's poetry comes not from an overflowing heart and as the result of an uncontrollable impulse. The element of will was a part of the creative urge, and the reader is conscious of this. His poetic idea was not carried on the flow of words but controlled it, so that the reader's attention is not carried on the flow of words either but is aware of their manipulation, and without careful attention to this can derive no satisfaction from the poems. George did not himself think that there was any break in his poetical development, nor indeed is there. His mission as a poet began with the aim of rescuing poetry from that effeteness which was prevalent in his youth, and in his mature years he directed that mission upon the civilization of his time, for he saw that poetry is an index of the age in which it is written.

Like Hölderlin he recognized that he was a poet in penurious times: 'Dichter in dürftiger Zeit'. But he did not ask himself, as Hölderlin did, to what purpose one should be a poet in such times. Or if he did, his answer was ready to hand: for the very reason that they are penurious. For he recognized the truth of Jean Paul's saying: 'No age is in such need of poetry as that which thinks it can do without it'. Like Hölderlin too he realized that the gods had abandoned men, and like him he sought to replace them. But his attempt to do so was fraught with even greater difficulties than that of his predecessor. Nor can it be maintained that his desperate effort to find a substitute for the gods was more successful than Hölderlin's. Like him too he feels himself to be the bearer of a message to his people; his aim is to form a community of those who share his ideals and to build a new society. That he should succeed in doing this to any wider extent was not to be expected; but amongst those he collected around him who were ready to carry his ideas out into the world—friends of similar aims in his youth and disciples in his mature years—were men of distinction in the world of literature and scholarship: Bertram, Gundolf, Norbert von Hellingrath, and some whose heroism brought them to their death by their defiance of the Nazi régime, such as Claus von Stauffenberg. Within its limitations George's was no mean achievement.

George's *œuvre* is grandly planned and carried out on the grand scale. But something is felt to be lacking in it. A walled city, it is laid out—like one of those German towns of the Renaissance which were planned with geometrical precision by some autocratic prince of the age—with gardens, open places, fountains and palaces, a temple surmounting all. About its streets goes one in singing robes extolling, acclaiming, admonishing, warning. We hear his voice but we rarely see him. The inhabitants stand in noble and heroic attitudes. But they neither move nor speak. For they are the sons not of Prometheus but of a Pygmalion to whom no divine boon has been granted. In fact they are statues, and one is the statue of a god.

APPENDIX

p. 17 Rejoicing in the fields, in the blessing of their new labour, ancestral father delved, ancestral mother milked, thus nourishing the destiny of a whole people.

p. 22 It was at the worst crossroads of my journey... On this side the districts which I avoided, so great was my disgust of everything which was praised and practised there. I mocked at their gods, they at mine. Where is your poet, poor and boastful people? There is none here.

p. 34 Ill-pleased she senses the pride of the things which have sprung up merely to bloom.

p. 35 I wanted it to be of cool iron and like a smooth, firm fillet; but in all the seams of the mine there was no metal ready to be cast.

Now therefore it shall be thus: like a great exotic flower-head, formed of fire-red gold and rich, flashing precious stones.

p. 37 Where no will functions except his own; and where he dictates to the light and the weather.

p. 37 My garden needs neither air nor warmth, the garden which I cultivated for myself; and the lifeless flocks of its birds have never beheld a springtime.

p. 42 Yonder on the shore a brother beckons, waving his joyous banner.

p. 43 Let us wander round the motionless pond into which the water-ways flow. You seek serenely to comprehend me. A wind blows round us, soft as spring.

The leaves which lie yellow upon the ground scatter a new perfume: in wise words you repeat what has gladdened me in the pictured book.

But have you knowledge also of profound happiness, have you understanding of the silent tear? Shading your eye you stand on the bridge watching the flight of the swans.

p. 43 The flower which I foster at the window protected from frost by the grey pot has long distressed me in spite of the care I take of it, and hangs its head as if it were slowly dying.

In order to remove from my mind the memory of its former blossoming I choose a sharp implement and cut off the pale flower with its sick heart.

59

Why should it serve to cause me bitterness? I wish that it should disappear from the window ... Now again I lift my empty eyes and in the empty night my empty hands.

p. 44 The year as it mounts fills the air still
With scents from the garden, though few,
Weaves in your fluttering hair still
Ivy and speedwell blue.

The waves of the wheat are like gold yet,
Perhaps not so full nor so free,
Roses to greet you unfold yet
Dimmed though their glory may be.

Say nothing of what is denied us
Let us vow to be happy, we twain,
Even though nothing more may betide us
Than to walk thus together again.

p. 45 My moist eyes seek only in the distance the One who gladly takes the rich and well-tuned harp—our golden harp.

p. 45 Do not feel terror at the threatening riddle of the icy glaciers; lift your questing glance to the earnest stars.

p. 47 But occasionally noble fire breaks forth from them and makes clear that union with them will bring no shame. Then say: in strong community of suffering with you I grasp your fraternal hands.

p. 49 To one you are a child, to another a friend. I see in you the God whom I recognized with awe, to whom I owe my devotion.

p. 52 I am the One and I am Both; I am the Procreator and the Womb, I am the Dagger and the Sheath; I am the Victim and the Blow.

p. 52 God's path is prepared before us
God's country is destined for us
God's war is ignited for us
God's crown is bestowed upon us.

p. 53 He who has once encircled the flame let him remain the flame's satellite, however much he may wander and stray. As long as its gleam reaches him he is not far from the goal. Only when his glance loses it, his own glimmer deceives him. If he lacks the central law he drifts and falls to pieces in the void.

p. 54 My suffering life approaches slumber; but the promise of the heavenly ones in its goodness rewards the piety of him who is not permitted to enter the Kingdom. I shall become the grave of

60

heroes, I shall become the turf which holy scions will approach for their fulfilment. With this the new age will come: love gave birth to the world, love will give birth to it anew. I have spoken the incantation; the circle is drawn; before darkness overtakes me I am carried away in high vision: soon the God on light soles will wander through the beloved fields, tangible in his glory.

p. 54 With all your arts you never learn what it behoves you most to know; but we serve in silence. Hear only this: destroying us you destroy yourselves. Only where our shaggy coat touches comes milk; where our hoof has not trodden no blade grows. If your intellect only had been at work your whole race would long since have been destroyed with all its doings. Your wood would have mouldered, your fields of seed would lie untilled. Magic alone keeps life awake.

p. 55 What I still think and what I still form, what I still love, bear the same features.

p. 55 You like a flame, you pure and slender.
You like the morning calm and bright,
Of noble stem you blossom tender,
You like a spring concealed and slight.

You walk with me in sunny meadows
Thrill round me in the evening haze
Illuminate my path in shadows
You cooling wind you burning blaze

You, all I wish and all I think of,
With every taken breath are blent,
I savour you in all I drink of
And you I kiss in every scent.

Of noble stem you blossom tender,
You like a spring concealed and slight,
You like a flame, you pure and slender,
You like the morning calm and bright.

BIOGRAPHICAL DATES

1868   Born at Büdesheim
1886-9   *Von einer Reise; Zeichnungen in Grau; Legenden*
         (Published under the title '*Die Fibel*' 1901)
1889   George in Paris
1890   *Hymnen*—limited edition
1891   Meeting with Hofmannsthal in Vienna
         Pilgerfahrten—limited edition
         Translations of Baudelaire—privately circulated
1892   *Algabal*—limited edition
1895   *Die Bücher der Hirten und Preisgedichte; der Sagen und Sänge;*
         und der Hängenden Gärten
1897   *Das Jahr der Seele*
1899   *Der Teppich des Lebens und die Lieder von Traum und Tod.*
         Mit einem Vorspiel
1901   Translations of Baudelaire augmented and published
1905   Translations of English and French poets
1906   *Maximin, ein Gedenkbuch*—privately published
1908   *Der Siebente Ring*
1909   Translation of Shakespeare's Sonnets
1912   Translation of passages from *La Divina Commedia*
1914   *Der Stern des Bundes*
1928   *Das Neue Reich*
1933   George leaves Germany for Switzerland
         Death at Minusio

SELECT BIBLIOGRAPHY

GUNDOLF, FRIEDRICH	*George*	1920
WOLTERS, FRIEDRICH	*Stefan George und die Blätter für die Kunst*	1930
DUTHIE, EDNA LOWRIE	*L'Influence du Symbolisme français dans le Renouveau Poétique de l'Allemagne*	1933
LACHMANN, EDUARD	*Die ersten Bücher Stefan Georges*	1933
KOCH, WILLI	*Stefan George—Weltbild, Naturbild, Menschenbild*	1933
MORWITZ, ERNST	*Die Dichtung Stefan Georges*	1934
LEPSIUS, SABINE	*Stefan George, Geschichte einer Freundschaft*	1935
MAIER, HANS ALBERT	*Stefan George und Thomas Mann, zwei Formen des dritten Humanismus*	1946
SALIN, EDGAR	*Um Stefan George*	1948
JAIME, EDWARD	*Stefan George und die Weltliteratur*	1949
BOEHRINGER, ROBERT	*Mein Bild von Stefan George*	1951
ASBECK-STANSBERG, LENI	*Stefan George—Gestalt und Werk*	1951

IN ENGLISH

BUTLER, E. M.	*The Tyranny of Greece over Germany* (Chapter 8)	1935
BOWRA, SIR MAURICE	*The Heritage of Symbolism* (Chapter—Stefan George)	1943

TRANSLATIONS INTO ENGLISH

SCOTT, CYRIL MAIER	*Selected Poems*	1910
VALHOPE AND MORWITZ	*Selected Poems*	1944